EVEREST
THE CRUEL WAY

EVEREST
THE CRUEL WAY
THE AUDACIOUS WINTER ATTEMPT OF THE WEST RIDGE

JOE TASKER

Vertebrate Publishing, Sheffield
www.v-publishing.co.uk

EVEREST
THE CRUEL WAY

Joe Tasker

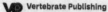 **Vertebrate Publishing**
Omega Court, 352 Cemetery Road, Sheffield S11 8FT, United Kingdom
www.v-publishing.co.uk

First published in Great Britain in 1981 by Methuen (London).
This edition first published in 2021 by Vertebrate Publishing.

Copyright © The Estate of Joe Tasker, 1982.

Front cover: Joe Tasker © Chris Bonington Picture Library.

The Estate of Joe Tasker has asserted Joe Tasker's rights under the Copyright,
Designs and Patents Act 1988 to be identified as the author of this work.

This book is a work of non-fiction based on the life, experiences and recollections of Joe
Tasker. In some limited cases the names of people, places, dates and sequences or the
detail of events have been changed solely to protect the privacy of others.

A CIP catalogue record for this book is available from the British Library.

ISBN 978-1-83981-052-7 (Paperback)
ISBN 978-1-906148-74-4 (Ebook)
ISBN 978-1-83981-070-1 (Audiobook)

10 9 8 7 6 5 4 3 2 1

Every effort has been made to obtain the necessary permissions with reference to copyright
material, both illustrative and quoted. We apologise for any omissions in this respect and will
be pleased to make the appropriate acknowledgements in any future edition.

Cover design and production by Rosie Edwards, Vertebrate Publishing.
www.v-publishing.co.uk

Vertebrate Publishing is committed to printing on paper from sustainable sources.

MIX
Paper from
responsible sources
FSC® C018072

Printed and bound in Great Britain by Clays Ltd, Elcograf S.p.A.

CONTENTS

FOREWORD: A GREAT PARTNERSHIP

by Chris Bonington

It was 15 May 1982 at Advance Base on the north side of Everest. It's a bleak place. The tents were pitched on a moraine, the debris of an expedition in its end stage scattered over the rocks. Pete and Joe fussed around with final preparations, packing their rucksacks and putting in a few last-minute luxuries. Then suddenly they were ready, crampons on, rope tied, set to go. I think we were all trying to underplay the moment.

'See you in a few days.'

'We'll call you tonight at six.'

They set off, plodding up the ice slope beyond the camp through flurries of wind-driven snow. Two days later, in the fading light of a cold dusk, Adrian Gordon and I were watching their progress high on the North East Ridge through our telescope. Two tiny figures on the crest outlined against the golden sky of the late evening, moving painfully slowly, one at a time. Was it because of the difficulty or the extreme altitude, for they must have been at approximately, 27,000 feet (8,230 metres)?

Gradually they disappeared from sight behind the jagged tooth of the Second Pinnacle. They never appeared again, although Peter's body was discovered by members of a Russian/Japanese expedition in the spring of 1992, just beyond where we had last seen them. It was as if he had lain down in the snow, gone to sleep and never woken. We shall probably never know just what happened in those days around 17 May, but in that final push to complete the unclimbed section of the North East Ridge of Everest, we lost two very special friends and a unique climbing partnership whose breadth of talent went far beyond mountaineering. Their ability as writers is amply demonstrated in their books.

My initial encounter with Peter was in 1975 when I was recruiting for the expedition to the South West Face of Everest. I was impressed by his maturity at the age of twenty-three, yet this was combined with a real sense of fun and a touch of 'the little boy lost' manner, which he could use with devastating effect to get his own way. In addition, he was both physically and intellectually talented. He was a very strong natural climber and behind that diffident, easy-going manner had a personal drive and unwavering sense of purpose. He also had a love of the mountains and the ability to express it in writing. He was the youngest member of the Everest team and went to the top with our Sherpa sirdar, Pertemba, making the second complete ascent of the previously unclimbed South West Face.

As National Officer of the BMC, he proved a diplomat and a good committee man. After Dougal Haston's death in an avalanche in Switzerland, he took over Dougal's International School of Mountaineering in Leysin. He went on to climb the sheer West Face of Changabang with Joe Tasker, which was the start of their climbing partnership. It was a remarkable achievement, in stark contrast to the huge expedition we had had on Everest. On Changabang there had just been Pete and Joe. They had planned to climb it alpine style, bivouacking in hammocks on the face, but it had been too cold, too great a strain at altitude, and they had resorted to siege tactics. Yet even this demanded huge reserves of determination and endurance. The climb, in 1976, was probably technically the hardest that had been completed in the Himalaya at that time, and Pete describes their struggles in his first book, *The Shining Mountain*, which won the John Llewelyn Rhys Prize in 1979.

Pete packed a wealth of varied climbing into the next few years. In 1978 both he and Joe joined me on K2. We attempted the West Ridge but abandoned it comparatively low down after Nick Estcourt was killed in an avalanche. In early 1979 Pete reached the summit of the Carstensz Pyramid, in New Guinea, with his future wife, Hilary, just before going to Kangchenjunga (the world's third highest mountain) with Joe, and Doug Scott and Georges Bettembourg. That same autumn he led another comparatively small team on a very bold ascent of the South Summit of Gauri Sankar.

The following year he returned to K2 with Joe, Doug and Dick Renshaw. They first attempted the West Ridge, the route that we had tried in 1978, but abandoned this a couple of hundred metres higher than our previous high point. Doug Scott returned home but the other three made two very determined assaults on the Abruzzi Spur, getting to within 600 metres of the summit before being avalanched off on their first effort, and beaten by bad weather on a subsequent foray. Two years later Pete and Joe, with Alan Rouse, joined me on Kongur, at the time the third-highest unclimbed peak in the world. It proved a long-drawn-out, exacting expedition.

Joe Tasker was very different to Peter, both in appearance and personality. This perhaps contributed to the strength of their partnership. While Pete appeared to be easy going and relaxed, Joe was very much more intense, even abrasive. He came from a large Roman Catholic family on Teesside and went to a seminary at the age of 13 to train for the priesthood, but at the age of 18 he had begun to have serious doubts about his vocation and went to study sociology at Manchester University. Inevitably, his period at the seminary left its mark. Joe had a built-in reserve that was difficult to penetrate but, at the same time, he had an analytical, questioning mind. He rarely accepted an easy answer and kept going at a point until satisfied that it had been answered in full.

Their climbing relationship had a jokey yet competitive tension in which neither of them wished to be the first to admit weakness or to suggest retreat. It was a trait that not only contributed to their drive but could also cause them to push themselves to the limit.

Joe had served an impressive alpine apprenticeship in the early seventies when, with Dick Renshaw, they worked through some of the hardest climbs in the Alps, both in summer and winter. These included the first British ascent (one of the very few ever ascents) of the formidable and very remote East Face of the Grandes Jorasses. In addition they made the first British winter ascent of the North Wall of the Eiger. With Renshaw he went on to climb, in alpine style, the South Ridge of Dunagiri. It was a bold ascent by any standards, outstandingly so for a first Himalayan expedition. Dick was badly frostbitten and this led to Joe inviting Pete to join him on Changabang the start of their climbing partnership.

On our K2 expedition in 1978, I had barely had the chance to get to know Joe well, but I remember bring exasperated by his constant questioning of decisions, particularly while we were organising the expedition. At the time I felt he was a real barrack-room lawyer but, on reflection, realised that he probably found my approach equally exasperating. We climbed together throughout the 1981 Kongur expedition and I came to know him much better, to find that under that tough outer shell there was a very warm heart. Prior to that, in the winter of 1980–81, he went to Everest with a strong British expedition to attempt the West Ridge. He told the story in his first book, *Everest the Cruel Way*.

Our 1982 expedition to Everest's North East Ridge was a huge challenge but our team was one of the happiest and most closely united of any trip I have been on. There were only six in the party and just four of us, Joe, Pete, Dick Renshaw and I, were planning to tackle the route. Charlie Clarke and Adrian Gordon were there in support going no further than Advance Base. However, there was a sense of shared values, affection and respect, that grew stronger through adversity, as we came to realise just how vast was the undertaking our small team was committed to.

It remained through those harsh anxious days of growing awareness of disaster, after Pete and Joe went out of sight behind the Second Pinnacle, to our final acceptance that there was no longer any hope.

Yet when Pete and Joe set out for that final push on 17 May I had every confidence that they would cross the Pinnacles and reach the upper part of the North Ridge of Everest, even if they were unable to continue to the top. Their deaths, quite apart from the deep feeling of bereavement at the loss of good friends, also give that sense of frustration because they still had so much to offer in their development, both in mountaineering and creative terms.

Chris Bonington
Caldbeck
September 1994

1 A STEP FURTHER

Everest has a magic which cannot be explained away. To the general public it is perhaps the only mountain which it is even partly comprehensible to want to climb. To a mountaineer, involvement with Everest can become obsessional. Our attempt, to climb the mountain by its most difficult route, at the worst time of the year and without oxygen, was the furthest point yet reached in the long history of Everest and in the story of a climber's need to explore the limits of what is possible.

After a chequered history of mistaken assertions regarding height and misnomers, the mountain we now know as Mount Everest or Sagarmatha became recognised in 1849 as the highest mountain in the world with a definitive height of 29,028 feet. It was seventy-two years after this that the first expedition to Everest was mounted. It took another thirty-two years before the summit was reached.

The first ascent in 1953 by Ed Hillary and Tenzing Norgay, members of the team led by John Hunt, was a turning-point in world mountaineering. Whatever controversy was to arise subsequently regarding the use of oxygen and size of expedition, the mountain which had defied all attempts for three decades was finally climbed and new vistas of what was possible in mountaineering were opened up.

It was ten years before the next major step forward on Everest took place. The American expedition under the leadership of Norman Dyhrenfurth succeeded in climbing the mountain by two routes. The South Col route was ascended in a conventional manner but Tom Hornbein and Willi Unsoeld made the audacious first ascent of the West Ridge from the Western Cwm and, abandoning their camps on the West Ridge, went over the top to descend the South-East Ridge in what is still regarded as one of the most committed and impressive achievements on the mountain. This ascent marked a switch away from a simple repetition of the established South Col route and a focusing of attention on more difficult and uncertain ways of reaching the top.

Each generation has to find and test its own limits; this is the only way of maintaining the vigour and intrinsic interest of the sport. The next problem on Everest to preoccupy mountaineers was the ascent of the difficult South West Face. Only after many attempts by large and very strong expeditions was this problem finally solved in 1975 by Chris Bonington's team. This expedition aroused, in its turn, much controversy beforehand for the futility of the exercise and the cost involved. Success silenced the critics and in retrospect it can be seen that not only did the expedition promote general public interest in mountaineering in this country, with positive benefits for many climbers, but it also liberated the climbing world from preoccupation with this one problem and gave credence to the pursuit of other improbable goals.

Thereafter the pace of exploration on the mountain increased. In 1978 Reinhold Messner, Peter Habeler and Hans Engel repeated the original route on the mountain but without the use of supplementary oxygen. They descended without any obvious, lasting ill-effects, and thus definitively demonstrated the feasibility of climbing any mountain in the world without oxygen. Mountaineers could now concentrate on finding the most demanding way of climbing a mountain rather than on how to transport great weights of oxygen equipment up to a certain point in order to guarantee success. At its most satisfying, mountaineering does not need the certainty of success, it needs a worthwhile objective reached against all the odds. The ascent of Everest without oxygen gave new life to the sport.

In 1979/80 the Poles, with their usual knack for choosing a formidable and punishing objective, were the first to mount an expedition to climb Everest in winter. After a long siege, they succeeded in climbing the original route, basing their tactics on their experiences on Lhotse in the winter of 1974/5. During that attempt they had experienced such savage weather conditions, cold, wind and snow, that they had felt that without life-giving oxygen support they would not even have been able to breathe. Officially their ascent of Everest is not recognised as a winter ascent by the Nepalese government as they actually reached the summit after the formal end of the season which, in Nepal, is held to be from the beginning of December to the end of January.

This is a very short season considering how much longer the climbing takes in winter due to the demoralising effect of the intense cold and, in the context of the Polish expedition, calendar dates count for little in classifying what is and what is not winter. There is no doubt that for the major part of their expedition the Poles were on the mountain in very 'wintry' weather.

1980 saw the stunning achievement of Reinhold Messner in climbing Everest on his own, without oxygen. Far from being exhausted, Everest was continuing to be the setting for revolutionary advances in mountaineering.

It does not take research to find something which is the 'next great problem' to tackle. We benefit from and profit by the achievements of others; it is as if a particular exploit passes into the experience of mountaineers as a whole and everyone's horizons are widened so that we see what is the next logical step to take. For the small team of us who formed ourselves together during 1979 and 1980, it seemed the most obvious thing in the world that we should now look to an ascent of Everest during winter, by its most difficult route and without oxygen. To any one of the many people who were to ask 'Why?' in the months preceding our departure, the only reply possible was: 'Because it is hard and because it is uncertain.'

We never achieve mastery over the mountains; the mountains are never conquered; they will always remain and sometimes they will take away our friends if not ourselves. The climbing game is a folly, taken more or less seriously, an indulgence in an activity which is of no demonstrable benefit to anyone. It used to be that mountaineers sought to give credence to their wish to climb mountains by concealing their aims behind a shield of scientific research. But no more. It is now accepted, though not understood, that people are going to climb for its own sake.

The reasons people climb are diverse, ranging from a simple satisfaction at physical exercise to a single-minded need to find ever harder and more punishing problems to solve. The central theme is one of testing the self to a greater or lesser extent at whatever level of the game we choose to play it. In the sense that it is unnecessary to play this game at all, climbing is a useless activity; in the context of discovering oneself, testing the limits of one's ability, exploring the boundaries of fear, determination and endurance, climbing is a means of self-fulfilment and a source of great satisfaction. The other delights of climbing as a way of life, the enjoyment of an outdoor environment, the simplicity of expedition life, the pleasure at being physically completely fit, are all bonuses beside this central theme.

For Reinhold Messner, the urge to test his own personal frontiers drove him to climb the 26,660-foot Nanga Parbat on his own. The same quest was to inspire the small group of eight of us to make plans to attempt Everest in the cruellest conditions imaginable, in winter.

2   THE IDEA AND THE TEAM

The thought of climbing Everest in winter had never entered my head. I had once finished an article on trends in mountaineering by mentioning the untapped potential of the Himalayas in winter, but my mind was occupied with other projects. In early 1979, with Pete Boardman and Doug Scott, I had climbed the third highest mountain in the world, Kangchenjunga, 28,208 feet, by a new route and for the first time without the use of oxygen equipment. Subsequently my thoughts were taken up with the return to K2, 28,253 feet, the world's second highest mountain. In 1978 a team of eight of us had attempted the difficult West Ridge, but we had abandoned the climb when our companion, Nick Estcourt, was swept to his death from 22,000 feet in an avalanche. In spite of the traumatic memories this mountain held for us, there remained the compulsion to climb it and a team of four of us planned a new attempt for 1980.

My days were filled, when back in Britain between expeditions, with a crazy mixture of ceaseless telephone calls, occupation with running a climbing equipment shop and endless preparations for the next expedition. Into my shop, the Magic Mountain, one day in the autumn of 1979 came Chris Bonington and Brian Hall, ostensibly shopping for gear of which Chris, after two-and-a-half decades of climbing, still does not seem to have enough. With Chris out of earshot, Brian quietly asked if I was doing anything during the winter of 1981/82 and, if not, would I be interested in going to Everest with a small group of people, which he and Alan Rouse were organising, to climb the West Ridge.

Inevitably Chris Bonington's name is associated with Mount

Everest, but he is representative of an older generation, with a more traditional approach to expeditions, having a formal leadership and hierarchical structure of command and organisation. By waiting until he was out of range of hearing, Brian was letting me know that he did not want Chris to know anything about the project. It was a non-verbal communication of the intention to form an expedition more along the lines of the successful expeditions we ourselves had grown accustomed to, lightweight in logistics, small-scale in terms of numbers and democratic in organisation.

Usually I have been involved with the planning of an expedition right from the start, or had a reasonable idea of the possibility of being invited. This invitation, however, came completely without warning. I had a moment in which to give a reply – Brian was getting a lift to the Lake District with Chris, who was in a hurry. I had a sensation of giddiness as the beauty of the idea, the breathtaking audacity of such a suggestion, hit me and at the same time a rapid vision of all the impossibilities – work involvements, lack of money, lack of time, personal relationships – the traditional dilemma of the climber, the conflict between his career, social life, love life, security and the fulfilment which comes from the all-absorbing commitment to some heady project. I gave Brian a quick 'yes' and agreed to speak with him later. A few days later I received from Chamonix a letter from Alan Rouse with details of their plans and a typed list, with my name and address already on it, of the eight members of the expedition. My consent had been taken for granted; asking was simply a formality!

The winter of 1981/82 seemed suitably far off, almost two-and-a-half years away, and I could comfortably shelve the idea until nearer the time. In the last eighteen months I had been away on three expeditions – nine months in total, hardly leaving myself time to unpack from one trip before re-packing for the next. My shop was being run on a chaotic basis, the days just not being long enough for all that there was to do, and I relied heavily upon the invaluable work of the shop's manager, Alf. There had already been one casualty in my private life as a result of my absence abroad, when I came back from the second expedition in six months, with a six-week period at home between the two trips, to find that my girlfriend had decided she had had enough of associating with someone whom she only saw every few months.

I was returning to K2 in the spring of 1980 and after that I planned to spend some time at home to concentrate on work and generally getting my affairs into some sort of order. A longish spell at home seemed very desirable, with even the possibility of finding the leisure to do some rock climbing which expeditions preclude. At the end of that spell was the enthralling prospect of Everest in winter, which I had not focused on clearly but which in the back of my mind I knew was the next logical step for me.

Some months after I was first invited we learnt that the winter period of 1981/82 was not available to us, making our options 1980/81 or some date five years hence. Suddenly the leisured approach to Everest vanished – a hard decision had to be made. The later date was hardly worth considering, for by then the route may well have been climbed, taking away some of the unknown element. The 1980/81 date, less than twelve months away, was a little too close and we would be hard pressed to raise the money and organise the equipment for then. For my part I was already committed to an expedition to K2 which, all being well, I would only be back from three months before going away again. Life was going a little too fast. It seemed clear that 1980/81 was the only sensible choice and, faced with a decision, I realised that it was all-important for me to go on the Everest winter expedition because it promised to be extremely hard, and improbable, the finest challenge in the sport that I could conceive of. It was so obviously the next logical step forward in mountaineering, to climb in the Himalayas in winter, that I felt the idea had been part of my consciousness for years. Come what may, I decided to go.

The team was to be made up of a small group of friends, most of whom had climbed together for a number of years. The birth of the original, daring idea was due to Alan Rouse and Brian Hall, who had taken part in a bold, lightweight ascent of the 25,300-foot Jannu in eastern Nepal. Both Alan and Brian had climbed all over the world with first ascents and impressive repeats to their credit, particularly in South America where they had spent many months. They had used their worldwide experience to start a guiding service which had the whole world as its territory.

Alan, in the early 1970s, had been representative of a volatile new generation of rock climbers. Whilst still in his early teens, endowed with a fine natural ability which was belied by his studious air of abstraction, he was instrumental in setting a new trend in climbing with the boldness of some of his ascents. Unusually for someone who excelled in one facet of the sport, he began to transfer his attention to the bigger mountains, disclosing a drive and imagination beneath the deliberately cultivated exterior of a person dedicated to enjoyment and anarchy. He seemed a complex character, able to engage in the most serious of discussions and gain the respect of people from all walks of life, yet sometimes finding himself inexplicably involved in the most outrageous of escapades. Whatever he embarked upon, he wanted to go to the limit with it. He had studied mathematics at Cambridge and one sometimes got the impression that he tolerated, good naturedly, conversations on any subject but that his mind was flying along at a rapid pace and that he could assimilate concepts and spit out answers with the speed of a computer. Attacking Everest in winter was an astonishing idea but it was typical of Alan's cheek that he should have come up with it.

For a number of years, Brian and Alan had been close friends, Brian providing a sound, organisational sense to counterbalance Alan's prolific ideas. There was a contradiction in Brian in that he had acquired a reputation for outlandish, wild behaviour but when he turned his attention to organising such a thing as an expedition, he displayed unsuspected responsibility and a forceful persuasiveness which ensured that his side of a job was always completed.

Alan and Brian had climbed in South America with the Burgess twins, Adrian and Alan, two of the climbing world's most colourful characters. Identical twins, tall, broad and blond, of Viking descent, seeming to have inherited their forebears' predilection for debauchery, they are known as strong and resourceful mountaineers, specialising in survival. Alan Rouse used to say of them that they were the best people he had ever met as companions on a mountain. They were an automatic choice.

Paul Nunn is a prominent figure in mountaineering, not least for his infectious laugh which accompanies each tale from his vast repertoire of anecdotes and tall stories. Paul has been an established figure in climbing since many of us could remember. There is a restless energy about Paul which sends him off every year to some part of the world on a filming, if not a climbing, assignment, and the same restlessness, the same determination not to miss anything that might happen, keeps him up till all hours of the night to be the last one to leave a pub or party. He has an endless capacity for conversing on any topic imaginable and, a wry scepticism about life in general. Paul, without being overweight, is a solid bulk. His massive hands wrapped round a mug of beer seem to demonstrate a strength of personality as well as of physique. His experience over many years covers most of Europe, the Pamirs, the Caucasus, the Karakoram and the Indian Himalayas. As a lecturer in Economic History, he has a respectability that many of us lacked, and Alan asked him along on account of his solid background as a mountaineer as well as his potential for raising sponsorship from local firms to whom he was well known.

Pete Thexton was asked to come as the doctor, but his unpublicised record of achievement in the Himalayan regions of Kulu and Garwhal hinted at a quiet determination and hidden strength. Physically Pete appeared small, but he was stocky and strong. He is one of those people who change in appearance each time one looks at them, leaving the impression that they have been totally underestimated. He was least known of all the team to any of the members but on paper, at least, if there was going to be anyone as doctor, Pete was as well qualified as any doctor we knew to appreciate the medical problems of high altitude and also take part in the expedition as a full climbing member. To an ambitious climber, though, the added burden of ministering to the sick was a potentially frustrating responsibility.

John Porter, half-American, half-English, lives in an out-of-the-way town on the west side of the Lake District. One of the mystery men of the climbing scene, appearing periodically to go off on an expedition, usually with Polish climbers, and achieving a high reputation for his persistence and ability, he had climbed in the Hindu Kush, in India, and South America.

If Alan Rouse was of a scientific temperament, John was of an artistic one, with all that that entails of vague dreaminess, and the ability to reproduce the apt quotation. He always has a puzzled air and the resigned acceptance of a person who does not capitalise on his opportunities because he is too preoccupied with more abstract thoughts to be concerned with the practicalities of life.

I had not climbed with any of the members of the team, except for a rock route in North Wales once with Brian, but I lived close to most of them and saw them frequently on social occasions. I can only presume from this that in selecting a team, Alan and Brian felt that I would be able to integrate successfully with everyone else.

Expeditions can be so arduous, the members living in such close proximity to each other, that it is vital to have a group of people who are able to get on with each other and work together. It is not essential that the team be made up of close friends; friendship and the ability to work together do not necessarily coincide. The bond which is formed by members of an expedition who have worked and struggled together goes beyond friendship, it is more akin to the relationship with a brother whom one knows intimately and accepts for all his faults as well as his good points and virtues.

I was interested at the prospect of forging the strong bonds of new friendship with seven people whom I knew and liked, and whose achievements I admired, but cautious too at the potential for discord that was contained in an enterprise which would throw us all together, for a long spell, under the most trying conditions.

1980 was a hectic year. We were faced with the problem of amassing the equipment and money for the winter expedition a full twelve months sooner than we had expected. Had it been another pre- or post-monsoon expedition it would not have been so much of a problem. The winter in the Himalayas, however, was a largely unexplored period for climbing and, from what little information we could gather, conditions would be much more unforgiving than at any other time of year. Our preparations would have to be rigorous and our equipment, as far as we could ensure, faultless.

The history of winter climbing in the Himalayas is very brief. The arrival of winter was generally felt to mark the end of the climbing season, as with the British attempt on the South West Face of Everest in 1972. After nearly two months of continual effort, by the middle of November the lead climbers were moving to establish their top camp close to the rock band. On reaching the site for Camp 6, it was impossible to pitch a tent in the prevailing wind and climbing on the Rock Band above was also out of the question. Dougal Haston looked round the corner of the buttress on to what had been regarded as an escape route, an easier option of reaching the summit, to find that in such wind there were no easy options. Without his oxygen mask he felt that he would not have been able to breathe.

They had gone to their limit and, although success had eluded them, they had the inner satisfaction of knowing that it was through no weakness on their part that they had not made it. This was the start of winter, and as John Hunt was to say of the expedition later, 'No one who has experienced the appalling conditions prevailing at high altitude in the Himalayan winter can doubt that Bonington's team stopped in their tracks at the ultimate limit of human achievement imposed for the time being, by natural forces.'

In winter the 'jet-stream', the high winds which blow at anything up to 130 knots, usually at altitudes of around 35,000 feet, drop to lower altitudes, taking in the upper reaches of the Himalayan peaks. Little is known about wind behaviour on the mountains in winter but the widest-held belief was that above 25,000 feet a mountain was taking the full force of the jet-stream, and severe disturbance due to turbulence would be felt below that.

It was into this jet-stream that Haston, Scott, MacInnes and Burke climbed on that November day in 1972, and against which they realised it was impossible to make any progress. Meanwhile, emphasising the contrasts of winter, Jimmy Roberts was sitting on the hillside of Kalipatar at 19,000 feet, watching the lead climbers through binoculars. Comfortable under a hot sun in a clear sky, he could not understand the reasons for the retreat. He could only see the tiny figures moving up or down; he could not tell that the temperature was perhaps -30 degrees Celsius to -40 degrees Celsius, nor that the wind was gusting at 100 miles per hour. The coming winter was a deceptive time of extremes.

Polish climbers, somehow setting their own standards outside the mainstream of the climbing world, were the ones who applied themselves directly to the problems of climbing in winter in the Himalayas. The performance of Polish climbers has long given cause for astonishment. They seem to have an aptitude for choosing bold, dangerous climbs that are often completed under duress and against great hardship. It seems fitting that it was the Poles who were the first to step into this punishing arena with their winter ascent of Noshaq, a 24,580-foot peak in the Hindu Kush, during January/February 1973.

They were well prepared in some ways, and learnt much during the expedition. They experimented with ointments as protection against the cold; they described the winds as being of hurricane force and temperatures ranging between -25 degrees Celsius to -50 degrees Celsius at night. With tents ruined by the winds and themselves worn out with fighting against them, they had given up hope of succeeding when they were blessed with a spell of fine, calm weather and reached the summit on the night of 13 February.

Some members suffered from frostbite but the expedition was an outstanding success. Already, on the way home from that achievement, they started planning their next winter expedition for 1974/75, only this time to Lhotse, 27,923 feet, the fourth highest peak in the world.

There they met the same harrowing conditions as on Noshaq. Three members had to return to Kathmandu due to illness and their inability to recover in the hostile climate of Base Camp. The rest fought a two-month-long battle against the wind and cold, finally being driven back only a few hundred feet below the summit by the unheralded arrival of a vicious storm. Without oxygen masks, like Dougal Haston, they felt that they would not have been able to breathe in the wind-driven snow. Their permit for the mountain expired on 31 December and, although they had come prepared for a long siege lasting until March, they had to withdraw or risk a total ban on their climbing in Nepal for a number of years.

From these few sources of information on winter mountaineering we were able to cull only an overall impression of an extremely bleak and hostile environment where daily existence was totally concerned with survival, leaving little chance of relaxation. Success seemed improbable, and if achieved it would only be through extraordinary hardship and persistence.

For me, once the dream had taken possession there was no other way; for friends and climbing colleagues, from the security of their own, more sane, future plans, the West Ridge of Everest in winter was a gruelling fantasy for which they expressed pity rather than admiration.

Early in 1980 we heard that the same team of Polish climbers had succeeded in climbing the South Col route up Everest on 17 February. They had applied the knowledge gained on the two previous expeditions to Noshaq and Lhotse, taken oxygen to assist them against the dreadful cold and winds, and through persistence against the most severe storms, finally reached the top.

The South Col route is the way the mountain was originally climbed and the way it has been climbed most often since. Sometimes it is disparagingly called 'The Yak Route', indicating its lack of technical difficulty and illustrating the stories of some expeditions only reaching the summit because the members are pushed or pulled up the route by their Sherpas, in much the same manner as the Sherpas treat their yaks, the local beasts of burden. However, in winter there is no easy way up Everest, or indeed up any mountain.

Once again the Poles were caught in the skeins of bureaucracy in that the permission to climb Everest only came through to them in December, so they were halfway through the winter before they reached Base Camp. The official definition of the winter season by the Nepalese Ministry of Tourism is from 1 December to 31 January. This left the Poles little time to complete their ascent. An extension was allowed to 15 February, and a further extension requested. A couple of extra days were allowed but not the full length of time desired. It was a fitting reward for their determination that the Poles reached the summit on the last day that they were allowed to climb upwards.

Due to the arbitrary definition of the 'winter season' there was some doubt cast upon their claim to have climbed Everest in winter, as the date on which the summit was reached officially fell outside the dates defining winter. Consequently, in official terms Everest was still unclimbed in winter.

Mountaineers have long grown accustomed to the rules governing expeditions to the Himalayas but it comes as a surprise to many people that to be allowed to attempt to climb a peak in any of the Himalayan countries one has to 'book' it, and pay a fee ranging from £50 to £60 for modest peaks of around 20,000 feet to approximately £1,000 for the giants of Everest or K2. This is only the first step towards the mountain. One has to agree to abide by all the rules governing behaviour during the expedition, whether it be not photographing strategic bridges or only climbing between the fixed dates of the season allotted.

To citizens of a country which has not been invaded for a thousand years, such sensitivity over border security is incomprehensible. To people who are accustomed to wandering over their own hills and those of neighbouring countries at will, charging a fee to climb a mountain seems ludicrous. The Himalayas, however, mark a natural frontier which spans some of the most sensitive borders in the world. Periodically, in times of confrontation, whole mountain areas are put out of bounds, and only gradually, as international relations ease, are foreigners allowed back into the mountain regions, and only then when hedged in by regulations and accompanied by a government-appointed officer.

We would, of course, think nothing of it if we heard the fee charged for booking Wembley Stadium. It might be objected that this took some building and the fee is therefore justified, but we also have natural resources which we are prepared to pay, for, whether it be underground caverns or stretches of wasteland and a ticket collector charging you for parking your car. The Himalayan countries are all poor countries who use the demand for one of their own natural resources as a means of raising revenue.

The prospect of making the first overall winter ascent of Everest was very appealing but there was no doubt in any of our minds that the Poles had done what they set out to do – they had climbed Everest at the worst time of the year, whatever arbitrary definition of season might be attached to it. For us there were enough unknowns about our own projected ascent not to feel that the Poles in any way exhausted our interest in the mountain. The West Ridge is the most difficult route yet achieved on the mountain. It had been climbed in its entirety only once before, by a large Yugoslav expedition, and we planned to climb it in winter and without oxygen, testing further the limits of the possible.

Our expectations of finding a suitable sponsor for the expedition were disappointed. We needed £15,000 in cash, a minute amount in comparison with most other expeditions to Everest, for which the cost more normally amounts to tens of thousands of pounds. The low cost of our expedition was due both to our reliance solely on our own efforts on the mountain, and to our intention to climb without supplementary oxygen equipment. The cost of oxygen equipment and the logistics involved in transporting it up the mountain add enormously to an expedition's budget. We would have Sherpas at Base Camp, a small group comprising Sirdar, cook, cook boy and mail runner. The Sirdar coordinates hiring and organisation of porters. The cook and cook boy relieve the expedition members of the more mundane tasks in order that they can concentrate on the climbing. Although the cost of hiring and equipping this Base Camp staff, along with equipping and paying our Liaison Officer, can add as much as one third to the budget of a small expedition, this cost is small in comparison to that of kitting out a team of Sherpas to act as load-carriers on the mountain.

Everest in winter did not fail to excite everyone's imagination, but in a period of extreme economic decline few firms felt that they could justify supporting a sporting venture when they were operating on a short working week or laying off many of their workers.

Alan was occupied with the task of raising money, spending much of his time on the telephone or meeting possible sponsors. Our hopes were raised and dashed time after time.

In the midst of all the preparations, I left for the expedition to K2 with two members from the 1978 attempt, Pete Boardman and Doug Scott, and Dick Renshaw, partner for much of my early climbing activities. In a way I could not concentrate fully on Everest until K2, 'The Savage Mountain', was safely finished with. It was an expedition lasting three-and-a-half months, at the end of which I emerged emaciated and exhausted after a prolonged assault which culminated in three of us, a few hours away from the summit, being buried in the middle of the night in an avalanche. It was as near to death and resurrection as I have been. When the horror of burial and suffocation was over, we spent three days slipping closer and closer to exhaustion as we fought for survival during the descent from the mountain.

I felt as if I had been to the brink of the abyss and looked over the edge; I felt purged by the experience. Rather than being deterred by the ordeal, I realised more clearly than ever before that climbing mountains was what I wanted to do. The reasons are not easy to define; the closest I can come to explaining them is that it makes me the person I am; going to the absolute limit of one's capabilities in anything is always satisfying.

My interest in Everest was not diminished, I had simply kept it dormant whilst I concentrated on K2. During the return from Pakistan my attention gradually centred fully on what was to come. Pete taunted me with comments on my folly at planning to leave again so soon, less than three months after our return. He had been on two expeditions the previous year and found it almost too demanding on his time and energy. This year he was planning a trek in the Himalayas. It was going to seem strange going on an expedition without Pete. We had hardly known each other before our two-man expedition to Changabang in 1976 when we had spent forty days completely alone together. Miraculously, our mutual assessment of each other's capabilities had proved accurate, and when we came out of our wilderness after the forty days we had not only realised a fantastic dream but had found a bond of friendship which, without words, could enable either one of us to anticipate the other's thoughts and reactions. It was to be the basis for further mountain ventures together.

Pete was disappointed that he had not been asked to come with us for the winter expedition. He had already been to the top of Everest once in 1975 with the South West Face expedition, and he said that he did not really want to go again, but he would have liked to have been asked.

For my part, in the absence of someone on our team that I knew well, I hoped that I would have the experience and maturity to accommodate to all the different personalities in situations of stress, without any of the abrasiveness which is sometimes inevitable in the process of getting to know a person's inner self.

Alan asked me to be co-leader in the U.K. with a view to raising sponsorship. Unlike the more traditional styles of expedition with a strict, authoritarian leadership structure, the expeditions we had all been involved with were organised on a much more democratic basis. If there was a leader, it was as if by rota. From the point of view of obtaining permission from the Nepalese government it was necessary to have the name of one person as leader; for contacting sponsors it is essential to have a leader or co-leader as spokesman. Amongst, ourselves we each regarded the task of every member as equally important. For my part, I was very relieved to be free of the burden of organising the equipment, a job which requires a great deal of paperwork and time – time being my most scarce resource. In my role as fund-raiser I set out to investigate the possibilities of making a film of the expedition and also to contact the main media outlets to arrange news coverage.

Exploring the prospects of making a film offered a new, interesting departure. Allen Jewhurst is a close friend and a director of Chameleon Films, which specialises in making independent adventure films. After some casting around to get the feel of the idea, I asked him to go ahead with arrangements to bring a film crew with us. The initial hope of raising money in advance, by selling the rights to a television company, came to nothing, but if a successful film was made we stood a chance of recovering some of our money afterwards.

I had known Allen for a number of years and greatly enjoyed his company. He had had a flirtatious relationship with the climbing scene since 1976 when he and his partner, Chris Lister, produced the film of the ascent of the Trango Tower. As a friend I was glad for him to come with us, but as a business man with his own company I had never quite understood him. He seemed to have some involvement with most aspects of the TV world, and if it was not him personally it was 'one o' me companies', as he was fond of saying in his broad London accent. The offices of Chameleon Films in Leeds seemed to be plush and elegant beyond the visible means of the company. Since I only ever visited his offices after dark, I was never sure if the whole operation was not somehow reminiscent of the film 'The Sting' in which the façade of a betting office is erected to defraud someone (albeit a crook himself), and that if I returned in daylight I would not find the premises under a totally different guise. In fact, the Chameleon offices are still very much there and the company has a reputation as a serious programme maker.

Allen was full of enthusiasm for the idea of making a film and he enlisted the services of Mike Shrimpton as cameraman and Graham Robinson for sound. Mike had done some rock climbing and had travelled to most places in the world on TV assignments. On meeting him I was impressed at his thoroughness and ready grasp and appreciation of points at issue. Graham was very quiet, had no experience at all of climbing, and a look of panic would cross his face when anyone asked him if he was really going to Everest.

From past experience I knew that the presence of amiable outsiders to the climbing team can help to prevent the pressures and tensions of expedition life from getting out of proportion, but it was a major worry that something might happen to one of the film crew, who inevitably would not have much experience of the mountains they would have to live in, in bitter conditions, for the best part of three months. It was worry for their own sakes and for the sake of the expedition as a whole which affected me, for if any one of them did have an accident it would seriously affect the morale of the rest of us. On the 1972 South West Face expedition, Tony Tighe, who was there simply to lend a hand round Base Camp, was killed during the final days of the expedition when a serac in the icefall collapsed on top of him. During the Polish winter attempt on Lhotse, Stanislaw Latallo, one of their film crew, died from exposure and exhaustion. There is danger all the time, and it is more likely to strike if one's attention is focused on something other than the conditions on the mountains.

Given these reservations, everyone on the team was keen to co-operate in obtaining the material to make the best possible film. Having 'outsiders' along, especially ones who are recording your every move and word, can be a cause of conflict in itself and an incentive to reticence. We hoped, however, that by being closely involved in the filming ourselves it would be 'our' film, the film crew would be an integral part of the team, and we would thus have the opportunity of making the best, most accurate and intimate film on mountaineering that had ever been made.

John Porter was occupied amassing the food we were going to take with us in what little time he had free whilst organising the Kendal Mountaineering Film Festival. Pete Thexton was left to his own devices selecting and collecting all the medical equipment, pills and medicines he thought we would need. Paul Nunn was away on the Royal Geographical Society Karakoram Project for a while and on his return he lent a hand with negotiations over the film contract and provided a central gathering point for all the equipment, food and medicine in his house in Sheffield, where his patient wife watched her home being overtaken by the creeping monstrosity of the expedition. The Burgess twins, Al and Ade, who had been absent in Canada during most of the preparations, were sentenced to drive around collecting and packing all the outstanding pieces of equipment which had not already arrived.

As the date of departure drew nearer, so the number of calls from the press, television and radio increased. Whenever I had to speak to them I found myself repeating, as if rehearsed, the same things; my mouth seemed to produce the words while my brain was preoccupied with a dozen other things. Talking about a climb before I had actually done it was something I had never felt easy about. There was an element of shyness due to the doubts I had about my own competence or ability to succeed on any particular climb. I preferred the attempt to be my own private affair, or something shared with my climbing partner, but in going to the Himalayas it becomes necessary to announce beforehand one's intentions in order to obtain permission from the government in question and also to raise the necessary finance. It was an uncomfortable feeling on the first expedition I was involved with to have to tell people a full year beforehand what our intentions were.

Everest still excites the public's imagination more than any other mountain and there is a fascination with the dangerous aspects of attempting to climb it. Without having set foot on the mountain, the climber setting out for Everest can be the focus of the dangerously seductive attention of the media. He is a modern-day gladiator whose fascination is that he is stepping into an arena from which he knows there is a chance that he might not return. This knowledge may be something that he would rather cope with privately but the arena which draws him, and the particular arena of Everest which was drawing us, is a public one and we had to accept the consequences.

After an interview in which I had been open and sincere, but which was one of many interviews in which I had been open and sincere, I would feel empty and a little drained. The words and conversation had not penetrated to my inner being, I had given a 'performance', thus protecting the real self inside. It made me uneasy to participate in exciting the interest of the public climb which involved all eight of us pushing ourselves to the limit and courting death for a sustained period of time. I would have preferred to be reticent about the whole enterprise but, without being rude, this was not possible, and at least cooperation would mean that the media would have the facts right.

Alan had suggested that half of the team went out at the beginning of November with all the equipment and food. They would sort out the formalities, clear customs and start walking with all the baggage and porters. The rest of us would fly out two weeks later, taking a flight from Kathmandu on a small plane to Lukla, an airstrip part way along the route of approach to Everest. The whole approach march can take up to eighteen days from leaving the road. Flying to Lukla would cut about ten days off the journey. Alan had felt that those of us who had been away once already that year probably needed a bit more time in Britain. As usual, things arise to fill the space available, and although the feeling, after all the equipment and food had gone with the first four on 3 November, was something like the calm after a storm, there were many loose ends to tie up.

I was relieved to be spared the full length of the walk-in. Usually it is a time for relaxing; most of the problems of organisation have been solved, life becomes a very simple one of walking, resting and a gradual focusing of the concentration on the mountain ahead. The formalities in Kathmandu, however, and all the petty tasks of buying local food, equipping the cooks and Sherpas of the Base Camp staff, are very demanding, and I felt that the four of us who were going later had been given the softer option.

Somehow, though, I regretted not leaving with the first four. They would be involved with the expedition right from the start, they would be getting to know each other and growing together, a vital part in forming the strong bonds which would be essential for us in working together on the mountain.

As a complete surprise came a phone call from No. 10 Downing Street – an invitation to lunch with the Prime Minister and her guests, the King and Queen of Nepal. I treated the call as a joke, thinking that some friends must be pulling my leg. I rang the number I had been given and sure enough the call was answered with 'Hello, Prime Minister's office'. I was due to fly to Nepal the day before the lunch date, but after consulting the other members it was clear that nothing would be lost by my flying out two days later. I was intrigued to pass through that well-known doorway.

Paul Nunn, Brian Hall and John Porter took the plane on Tuesday 18 November. I spent the remaining time in London making final arrangements with *The Observer*, to which we would be sending back news reports, and similarly with ITN. I had discussions with a publisher who was interested in the story of the expedition and from Pentax I picked up an enormous 6 x 7cm camera which they were loaning to us for the expedition.

On the Wednesday I was running down Whitehall, late for the luncheon appointment, and hurried through the security checks outside 10 Downing Street and in through the door. It was as if I had stepped into Dr Who's time-ship, the 'Tardis'; outside it is a small, old-fashioned police box, inside it is enormous, exceeding, in some scientific fantasy, all proportions of the external shell. We are familiar with the little door of No. 10, with the policeman outside, resembling the entrance to a small terraced house. Inside, staircases lead up and down, passageways branch off in all directions; there are innumerable doors, antechambers, spacious gathering places and a large dining hall. I shook hands with Mrs Thatcher, who appeared and spoke exactly as on television. The King and Queen of Nepal seemed tolerant of the ritual introductions, a formality which they were having to repeat throughout their stay in Britain. With relief I recognised a familiar face, John Denson, the British Ambassador to Nepal, who had welcomed us back from our success on Kangchenjunga with a champagne toast at his embassy residence. The meal was conducted at a brisk pace, the whole procedure obviously orchestrated by a master of ceremonies to fit in with the Prime Minister's busy schedule. Politely but firmly the meal was brought to an end and there was an irresistible momentum to leave. I stepped out on to the street, saying goodbye to the Densons and promising to visit them in Kathmandu, and rushed off to complete the thousand remaining things I had to do before leaving.

3   GOING TO THE WIDOW MAKER

Three months after returning from the expedition to K2 I was at Heathrow airport again, ready for another departure. One of my sisters, Carmel, her fiancé, Andy, and my girlfriend, Maria, were there. It was a strange parting. I was frantically re-packing, trying to avoid excess baggage charges; there was a delay whilst some ticket confusion was cleared up in the queue in front of me, and when it was my turn the flight had closed and there was a chance I might not get on. I rushed from one desk to another guided by idiotic, mistaken directions. My single-minded preoccupation with expeditions over the past months had been distressing to Maria, who felt very much incidental to my climbing plans. Now at the last moment there was no time to talk. I was at last checked in and we ran up the escalator before the final turn round for the goodbye, having hardly conversed for the hour we had been at the airport. Maria had a suddenly tearful and drained face – so much was left unsaid before I turned to go through the hole of an entrance as if to execution.

I do not feel lonely on an expedition, and I do not feel a dread of separation. An expedition is all-absorbing and fulfilling. I have known more loneliness in a city than on a remote mountain where I have been absolutely alone for a week, with not even the sight of another person. On a mountain I have an identity, a purpose and a place within the lives of other people. If there are times when one is physically alone it is not through any personal rejection, but because a vital role is being performed.

It was a relief to settle into my seat on the plane knowing that I was at last rejoining the mainstream of the expedition. For the last two weeks I had felt uncomfortably separated from the members of the expedition who had gone on ahead. There were innumerable things that I had not sorted out before leaving, many letters I would have to write from Kathmandu, but already the discord due to diverse, competing demands was beginning to fade away. By the time we reached Base Camp the whole pace of life would have slowed down and life itself become very simple.

On the flight from Delhi to Kathmandu I had a view of the snowy mountains we had come to climb. They seemed more snowy than in summer, but it was not white everywhere; at least we would not be on snow all through the approach march too.

I joined Paul, Brian and John in Kathmandu, that amiable city, which was a staging post for us in our transposition, from one culture to another. We flew on to Lukla, from where we walked for two days, in easy stages, to Namche Bazaar, where we hoped to meet the rest of the team.

The woods through which we walked were still mellow with the colours of autumn, in the shade there were patches of frost and at night the air was distinctly chill. From a clearing in the woods on the way up to Namche Bazaar we caught our first glimpse of Everest peeping menacingly above the crest of the Nuptse ridge. A huge plume of cloud streamed from the top, a chilling indicator of the power of the winds we were coming to face. Like a vision, the sight disappeared as we continued upwards through the trees, to be glimpsed again only briefly before we were much closer to the mountain; but the memory remained to haunt our imaginations as a warning of what was ahead.

We seemed to have been thrown into a way of life for which we were ill-prepared. Our progress from Britain, by aeroplanes which finally deposited us in the heart of the mountains, had been too rapid to allow time to adjust. I had a great sense of culture shock, feeling a little numbed mentally. At night it was very cold and all our warm clothing was still with the advance party who were some days delayed. We stayed in a travellers' rest house in Namche Bazaar, awaiting the arrival of the rest of the team.

Namche Bazaar is one of the main villages of the Sherpas,

members of the tribe of Tibetan origin who, turning from trade to agriculture, have become world famous for their mountaineering feats, for their endurance and reliability. This hillside village is a centre for commerce, whereas the other villages above and further up the valley are located in places where agriculture is more feasible. The whole area has been adopted by New Zealanders who, taking their example from Ed Hillary, have organised the area on a national park basis, introducing measures designed to conserve wood and prevent soil erosion. Their efforts are met by a mixed response from the local inhabitants, but there is no doubt that they have been effective in bringing education and medical care to the area.

I went to visit Ang Phurba, who had been Sirdar or chief Sherpa on our expedition to climb the north side of Kangchenjunga in 1979. He was a laconic but totally reliable and resourceful complement to our team. On a visit to Britain at the end of 1979 his first quest was to find a broad-brimmed cowboy hat such as he had seen me wearing on the expedition. He was at home with his wife and three children, relaxing during the winter months. Expeditions for him were over until the spring, the work in the fields was all finished and he could pleasantly pass the time with that philosophical calm of people in the east.

Like most of his fellow Sherpas, Ang Phurba is an able worker on an expedition, but has no interest in climbing for its own sake. With a record of expeditions which many of us would envy, he regards his climbing activities simply as work for which he gets paid. The attitude of the Sherpas to the visits of foreigners was summed up by a conversation which was translated for us in which it was made clear that we were regarded as reincarnated beings. In our former lives we were believed to have been so bad that we had been sent back into these mountains as a punishment. Had we behaved ourselves formerly we would have found ourselves in a much more comfortable setting! Ang Phurba and I drank chang, the Sherpa rice beer, and chatted about mutual friends. The centrepiece of the room was a wood fire, and lining the walls were huge copper bowls used to store water during the winter months when outside all is frozen.

Ang Phurba's home was unconventional in having a chimney above the open fire. For some reason the idea of chimneys does not seem to have made an impact on the Sherpas. Intelligent and resourceful as they are, the Sherpas seem to adapt to cold and discomfort rather than taking measures against it. It is not unusual to see a fire stoked up high with a cluster of bodies around it and windows and doors wide open to let some of the smoke which fills the room escape. It was not clear whether the common belief was that the smoke preserved the wood inside the houses (which were indeed blackened and festooned with sooty fronds) or whether it was to keep heat from escaping along with smoke up a hole. For whatever reason, Sherpas, and especially the women, spend their lives crouched, with smarting eyes, over smokey fires, and often have irreparably damaged eyesight by the time they are in their thirties.

The nearby hospital in the village of Kunde is staffed by voluntary doctors from New Zealand and is supplied largely with copious medicines from the many expeditions which pass by. It was built as part of the welfare scheme, started by Ed Hillary, providing hospitals and schools throughout the Sherpa villages. This hospital is a model of airiness, insulation and efficient heating.

For some reason the Sherpas do not take example from this; they continued to huddle, snivel-nosed, through the winter months in their dark and draughty, smoke-blackened rooms.

The hospital was to be our link with the outside world. Twice a week the New Zealand doctors send out their mail on a tiny Pilatus Porter aeroplane. The plane lands on an airstrip resembling a football field tilted at a considerable angle, poised above a deep valley. The flight into and out of this airstrip is spectacular and exhilarating. It was built to service the Japanese Everest View Hotel, a luxury hotel built in a position on a hill from where one can just see the summit cone of Everest. Everyone who stays at the hotel flies in, but the sudden jump up from the 5,000 foot altitude of Kathmandu to nearly 11,000 feet is often too much. It is not unknown for death to occur after such a rapid transition. Many of the visitors have to be met off the aeroplanes and supported all the way to the hotel where they collapse within reach of an oxygen bottle, with which every room is equipped, and stay there till their departure.

From Base Camp we would be sending back once a week our mail runner who would deliver his mail bag to the hospital. There it would be put on the plane from which it would be collected on arrival in Kathmandu by our expedition agent, who would then stamp and supervise the posting of mail, despatch of news film and cabling of newspaper reports. A long chain of communication, but we could sometimes have mail back in Britain within a week of sending it from Base Camp.

On 27 November Alan and Pete arrived with thirty of the porters they had hired to carry our 150 loads. By this time we had been waiting anxiously for several days, but the reasons for the delay were now explained. The Japanese expedition that would be attempting the normal route on Everest, effectively on the opposite side of the mountain, had hired 800 porters. This virtually cleared out the villages of available manpower, since much of the local workforce was already taken up with a new road-construction project. What villagers were available to carry for us were only prepared to go a certain distance, being unwilling to cross the mountain ridges separating their known, home valley from the next valley along the way. This entailed a constant paying-off and rehiring which in the end caused the porter caravan to be divided up into smaller, more manageable groups. Alan and Pete had come on ahead with the first group to let us know what was happening.

We moved up from Namche Bazaar to the more secluded village of Khumjung where we hired a house in which to stay, store all our baggage and find some privacy from the constant questions of the trekkers who frequent Namche Bazaar. There were few trekkers about; those that were about were well wrapped up, shocked by the cold and full of questions about our expedition. There was no two-way conversation; they seemed so overawed by the thought of climbing Everest that they did not offer anything of themselves; they were probing, searching for our motivation, our experiences, our fears. It was embarrassing and irritating to be such a focus of attention, and it became a habit with us to retreat into the isolated world bestowed by the stereophonic headphones of the little cassette players we had. This blocked out all outside sound so that, in the most selfish way, one could be obliviousof any conversation going on.

We learnt from Alan and Pete some of the tales of the walk in; the Burgess twins, nicknamed, for their propensity for carrying heavy loads, after two well-known rucksack manufacturers, Berghaus and Karrimor, racing along in competition with each other up and down hill. The porters loved them and mimicked their muscle-bound walk, striding along, arms akimbo, pretending to carry a cassette player which one or other of the twins seemed to have eternally glued to his hand, playing Blondie or some punk rock alternative at full volume.

We discussed tactics on the mountain, whether it would be best to climb as two groups of four or some other variation. Brian evolved a theory concerning the wind direction, and deduced that we could be assisted by the wind as it would be coming from behind, and that it would be so strong that more oxygen than normal would be blown up from below. Alan seemed to think that the colder air of winter would be denser, thus containing more oxygen and effectively lowering the height of the mountain in air-density terms.

The delay we were experiencing, although allowing those of us who had not walked in a chance to acclimatise, was worrying and we were all relieved at the arrival on 30 November of the infamous Burgess twins and the film crew of Allen, Mike and Graham.

Although clearly on unfamiliar territory, the approach walk of the last two weeks had enabled the film crew to accustom themselves to the primitive mode of existence that they were to share for the next couple of months. Their professional conditioning to keep on filming whatever the circumstances had helped them to adjust quickly to the strange environment and their methodical organisation had been invaluable in assisting with the marshalling of over a hundred unruly porters. The actual filming arrangements for the mountain had not yet been finalised. Mike was keen to go as far as he could but, since his climbing experience was limited, we were reluctant to make any commitments about whether we would be willing to have him working on the mountain at all in case it meant assigning someone to look after his safety. There was a definite pecking order in that the film was clearly regarded as secondary in importance to climbing the mountain and consequently the opinions of the film crew tended to be regarded with less weight. On the whole I did not envy them their work, which would inevitably entail their spending much time inactive at Base Camp. Even if Mike was to come part way up, the main filming on the mountain was expected to be done by the climbers.

Officially we were allowed to set foot on the mountain from the first day of December, and days lost early in an expedition are hard to make up later. I found myself regarding this reunion of the whole team as the real start of the expedition. Previously we had all been scattered with no chance of interaction, but once together we could begin to share ideas and form a close-knit team which would be effective on the mountain.

We were five days from Base Camp, and we left Khumjung before our Sirdar, Dawa, arrived with the remaining thirty loads. He, being well known in the region, had been left to bring up the rear.

The trail led steadily upwards, habitation and vegetation grew more sparse and the little comforts of life which had been gradually diminishing were pared almost right away as we drew closer to the mountain.

I walked along one day with Ade Burgess, discussing how it had been for us on Kangchenjunga and K2, what it was like to be so high without oxygen support equipment on those mountains. Undeniably it had been arduous but it had not been another dimension of experience; it was more of the same excruciatingly hard work. On Kangchenjunga three of us had spent a night in a snow cave at 26,000 feet, climbing the next day the 2,000 feet to the summit and descending, in the night, to the same snow cave. It had not been a fight against an unwilling spirit; inside I knew I wanted to continue, but like an old man whose mind is still active when his strength is failing, the question was whether my body could perform all the necessary movements to reach the summit before dark. Every half-dozen steps upwards left us panting, gasping in lungfuls of rarefied air. We had reached the summit one hour before dark, without hallucinations, without distorted perception or dizziness. The only indication that our brains were affected by the altitude was that we did press on to the summit, in the face of a rising storm, knowing that we would inevitably get benighted.

Next day I walked along with Al Burgess, only identifiable from his brother by the stubbly beard which gave him a mischievous appearance. We talked again of high altitude, K2 and Kangchenjunga. Al and Ade are quite different in temperament, outlook and even in some ways in their appearance, but these differences are only noticeable as one gets to know them both better. Even then, after not seeing them for a while, it is easy to mistake one for the other. In talking to one or other of them I usually felt a certain air of uncanniness, as if each one knew already what had been discussed with the other. As I talked again of K2 and Kangchenjunga, I could not help feeling that Al already knew what I was going to say, and that he had possibly only forgotten that I had already said these things the day before.

There is such a sense of togetherness in their awareness of each other, their intimate knowledge of each other, that the twins give an impression of strength that any union of separate parts gives. The girlfriend of one of them said that it is disconcerting to have a close relationship as no woman will ever be as close to either of them as they are to each other.

In the few days of preparations in Kathmandu, Al had met a girl who had become quite fond of him. She was planning to come up to meet him after we had finished on the mountain. We were planning to get Ade to grow a beard and impersonate his twin brother, with us in collusion calling him Al, to see how long it would take her, if at all, to spot the trick.

We left the village of Pheriche, climbing steeply up a narrow valley, enclosed by snowy mountains. At a col we passed a row of cairns, which stand, ominous as tombstones, to the memory of the Frenchman and five Sherpas who were swept away by an avalanche in their attempt to climb the West Ridge of Everest in 1974.

Lobuje is the last inhabited place on the way up to Everest. It consists of a few yak herders' dwellings which are now occupied on a more consistent basis, catering for the trekkers who make it this far. A saying which has come into use is, 'See Lobuje and die', a dictum arising from the dangers inherent in this trek. Lobuje is at approximately 14,000 feet and to the unwary or unfit the possibility of a fatal attack of high-altitude sickness is very real. A small hospital has been built by the Japanese at Pheriche, the last village on the trail, specifically to care for the visitors who become sick.

Each day now we were only walking for a few hours. It would have been possible, but unwise, to do more. The height gain between each stage was considerable and at this altitude it is the going up high too quickly which causes high-altitude sickness. In 1978 I had visited this area on the way to Nuptse, the third peak of the Everest massif, when one member of our team became critically ill at Lobuje. We carried him down to Pheriche 1,500 feet lower where he was cared for by a Sherpani girl. He recovered and subsequently married the girl. The story is legendary in this area, the fairytale fantasy of a rich stranger carrying off his true love having been given credence by this event.

Unlike the mountain folk of India and Pakistan, Sherpa society is delightfully open and relaxed. It was possible to laugh and joke with the womenfolk, something unheard of in Pakistan. A tea house at Lobuje was run by a Sherpa girl, fluent in English and French. We spent an evening sitting, with eyes smarting from woodsmoke, drinking chang and playfully flirting with the Sherpa girl and her friends. Everyone does much manual labour in this hill society, carrying heavy loads and tilling the fields. Even the women are very strong and any attempt at going further than their rules of decorum permitted was firmly rebuffed. They were fascinated by our two blond clones, the Burgess twins. Blond hair is unknown among the Sherpas, and this together with the twins' incredible size in comparison with the diminutive Nepalese people and their similarity made an obvious focus for the giggling attentions of the easy going Sherpanis.

The girl running the tea house knew Samji, the girl who had married my expedition companion.

'Samji my friend. You want to marry Sherpani like her?'

'In England we have "one night marriage", what about that?'

'One night no good, all night very good,' and she would relapse into ribald convulsions of laughter with her friends.

Gorak Shep was the last camping place before Base Camp. We pitched our tents on the sandy bed of a dried-up lake. From the hill behind it is possible to see Everest and we took it in turns to wander up for the view. I waited till late in the afternoon to catch the sunset on the mountain and sat for a freezing hour, growing progressively more numb in the chill breeze, recording the exquisite change of colours – from pink to deep orange – on Everest and the hills around. There did not seem to be much wind this day, but now the mountain looked huge and I was numbed with cold on a lowly hillock watching the sun slip away from the summit 12,000 feet higher.

We had a bleak, windswept evening meal, raked by sand from the dried-up lake bed, with the food congealing on the plates before there was time to finish eating.

We reached Base Camp on 6 December, end of one mode of existence and start of another. The winter snows had not lingered.

Our tents had to be pitched on the icy desert of the lower Khumbu glacier. Rocks churned up by the imperceptibly moving river of ice littered the surface. We spent a whole day hacking platforms from the ice and pitching tents with rocks to which we tied the the guylines. It was worth the effort to make each tent site comfortable as we expected to be there for many weeks.

To the north the camp was overlooked by the steep walls leading up to the Lho La, the lowest point on the West Ridge, and the complex slopes leading up to the West Shoulder, 6,000 feet above us. In 1978 I had seen an avalanche break away from the walls of ice guarding the Lho La, sweeping down in seconds and covering our camp, over a mile distant, with fine snow. Anything in its path would have been obliterated. I had thought then that any attempt to gain the Lho La was suicidal, but the Yugoslavs had found a cunning, though difficult, route up the rock buttresses to the left, avoiding most of the danger. We intended to follow this safer line.

4   ATTACKING THE RAMPARTS

The weather was fine and clear but definitely chilly, even on the sunniest day. It was hard to relax for long, for the cold penetrated right to the core. Paul Nunn, Pete Thexton and Alan Burgess were sick with dysentery or some related illness. We had thought to escape such illness in the sterile atmosphere of winter but the watering place for our last camp at Gorak Shep had been a stagnant pool and we suspected this to be the cause of the trouble. Only during the daylight hours between 8.30 a.m. and 4.30 p.m., if the sun was out, was there any semblance of warmth; those who were ill had little encouragement for recovery from our chill surroundings. Paul steadfastly refused Pete's panacea for dysentery-related illness, the much feared Flagyl, the effect of which was sometimes more debilitating than the illness for the three days of the dosage. Paul, having gathered on his travels much experience of strange illnesses, preferred to try to cure himself in his own way. Almost all of us had colds, snuffles and coughs.

Alan was preoccupied with the tedious task of paying off our porters, calculating the expedition's expenditure and ensuring that we had enough cash available in Nepalese rupees for all our expenses until returning to Kathmandu.

John Porter, having shelved his responsibility as food organiser during the confusion of the approach walk, now got down to the task of locating and making available the rations and the delicacies designed to make Base Camp life enjoyable.

Brian Hall continued his never-ending work of sorting out and distributing the equipment which he had worked so hard to design and amass specifically for this expedition. Everything had to be accounted for; if there was anything lost or forgotten there was little chance of replacing it before the end of the expedition.

Al and Ade Burgess and I were privileged to be free to make the first exploratory steps towards finding a safe route up the 2,000 feet of rock to the Lho La.

It was only meant as a reconnaissance, we wanted to find the point at which we left the glacier, so we went only in light clothes and light footwear. We hugged the edge of the glacier, hopping along the piles of unstable boulders, thrust to one side by the movement of the glacier. We risked breaking an ankle or worse if a boulder should roll over, but by skirting the edge we were keeping safely away from the fall line of the seracs, the walls of ice tilting forward from the Lho La, the debris from which lay scattered across the glacier.

I was a little breathless, unaccustomed as yet to the altitude of 18,000 feet. I did not want to show my breathlessness to the twins, who are always fit as a result of their constant training sessions all the year round. Implicitly I was weighing up my partners, and felt that I was being evaluated too in terms of performance and ability. There was an unspoken bravado and tongue-in-cheek banter which seemed to acknowledge the folly of our chosen pursuit. I revelled in the company of these two brothers, feeling in no way excluded from the rapport which they had with each other.

The sun warmed the rock and, unhampered by rucksacks or heavy, warm clothing, we found ourselves scampering further and further up the gradually steepening hillside.

We had heard that this approach to the Lho La was threatened, if not by ice avalanches, then by rock avalanches. Doug Scott and Georges Bettembourg had made a foray up these slopes in 1979 and came back with awestricken tales of the lethal rockfall that showered down out of the walls above. There was indeed much evidence of newly fallen rock and no trace at all that anyone had been here before, causing us to doubt if we were heading in the right direction.

There were several buttresses of rock separated by wide gullies full of loose stones and unstable blocks. We rushed across the gullies, fearing to be caught in them by fresh falls of rock, seeking the safety of the buttresses which stood out from the slope clear of the danger. Ade climbed up the side of one buttress thinking he had seen the obvious way up; Al and I tried another way. Once through an area of broken blocks and round a corner, we found we were on a logical progression of ledges, steps and ribs. Ade, having reached an impasse, stayed below, sheltering under a bulge of rock lest we dislodge any stones whilst climbing above him. Underfoot there was much loose rock and we realised that for safety any of us coming up here would have to stay close together. Like this, any rock dislodged could be either stopped or avoided more easily. If we were separated by long distances, anything dislodged would have a chance to gain lethal momentum and possibly strike the unwary without warning.

There was still no indication that the line we were taking would lead to the plateau of the Lho La. We were gaining height steadily, Base Camp was a tiny cluster of tents in the distance from which the echo of a voice sometimes reached us, and the hidden valley of the Western Cwm was gradually revealing itself. We were getting close to the huge walls of ice which guard access to the plateau, but in safety, to one side, we were able to look on with respect at the tortured ice formations frozen in the act of toppling over. This wall of ice, hundreds of feet high, was the end of a great bed of ice sitting on top of the rock of Everest's West Ridge. The rock is at a gentle gradient and the layer of ice is in gradual movement, slowly and inexorably sliding to the precipice beside which we were climbing. As it reaches the edge, great chunks, weighing thousands of tons, break off and crash down, scouring the gully below, and rising in a billowing cloud of ice debris which obliterates all in its path. Such avalanches are one of the nightmares of Himalayan climbing. I felt a reverential awe in gazing upon the birthplace of such colossal forces.

Al and I chased each other up the buttress; which after a jumble of loose shale, broken blocks and razor-sharp flakes had changed as we got higher to firm granite which was a pleasure to climb.

'It's like following a goat,' Al shouted up to me as I disappeared from his sight and found we could continue even further. I did not feel as fit as a goat but could move rapidly for short lengths of time before becoming breathless. I knew that if we did too much we would exhaust ourselves and probably spend the next day recovering from headaches. It was so exciting, however, this journey of discovery, that it was impossible to resist going just that little bit further.

A steep, difficult-looking corner blocked the way, but above it the angle of the rock eased back. Al gingerly edged his way up, spreading his legs wide and balancing his toes on small rugosities in the rock. In Britain it would have been the sort of climbing we could do without thinking; here on Everest we could not help but be influenced by the situation, climbing unroped at 19,000 feet, with the debris of danger lying all around. This instilled more caution than the difficulties justified. Al found some good handholds, pulled himself on to easier ground and I followed.

A ramp led upwards to a level shoulder on the crest of the buttress and a couple of rusty tin cans. It was an encouragement that we were going the right way. A nasty looking gully of loose rock and snow separated us from some grey slabs and at the top of the wall above us we could see a line of weakness, a groove or corner, which seemed to end after about 300 feet on the Lho La plateau. It was far enough for the day. A slight breeze cooled away the warmth of the sun; without lingering further we turned to descend.

On the way down we built cairns from small rocks to mark the way for the next time we came up. Down below Ade was waiting, chilled to the bone in his light clothing. Al and I been warm enough, moving all the time. Ade had been crouched in the shadow of the bulge of rock for an hour, as we, heedless of time, had gone much further than intended. United once more, we stumbled and slid down the unstable boulders to the glacier.

From above we had noted the way back to camp across the ice. This would mean crossing the avalanche debris from the ice walls of the Lho La, but we judged that we ran a greater risk of serious injury by staying on the boulder field. Many of the boulders were precariously balanced and big enough to crush a foot or break a leg if dislodged. It took ten minutes to rush across the hard packed avalanche cone to where we guessed ourselves to be out of danger, all the while spying crevasses into which to jump and shelter should an avalanche come sweeping along.

We brought the good news of our progress back to a camp busy with activity. Brian, sleeves rolled up, pad in hand, was surrounded by boxes from which were spilling out ropes, stoves, tents and umpteen other items of equipment which he was ticking off against a list and trying to organise into readily identifiable heaps. John, dressed in strange green padded pyjamas, strutted about with a continually worried air from one pile of food to another. He broke away periodically to try to explain, with an expression of resigned patience, to Wan Chup, our cook, what each sort of food was for and how to cook it.

There seemed to be many things missing or mislaid, and the thrill I had felt at our day of discovery disappeared as we became caught up in the mundane tasks of Base Camp organisation. After searching repeatedly through kitbags and boxes many things were unaccounted for. We questioned ourselves first, our own disorganisation, but too many vital pieces of clothing and equipment, jacket, trousers, ice axe, were missing from different loads for it to be a coincidence. Inevitably suspicions arose about the honesty of our Sherpa staff.

In order to be free to concentrate on the climbing, and also to look after Ram Singh, our Liaison Officer, we were hiring a cook, Wan Chup, who, according to the Nepalese laws of stratification, had to have a cook boy, Mingma. We also employed another Mingma, who was to be our mail runner. To look after this group and to organise porters or yaks and any transactions with the local community we had to have a Sirdar, or head Sherpa. This was the role of Dawa, whom we had left to bring up the rear with the remaining loads.

We were completely in the hands of our Base Camp staff, as we could not keep a check on all our equipment all of the time. Fortunately Nepalese generally and the Sherpas in particular have a high reputation for honesty. On Kangchenjunga to we had handed over the money to Ang Phurba, our Sirdar; and he had hired and fired the porters as necessary; presenting us with a detailed, if crudely written, set of accounts from time to time. We therefore struggled against admitting to ourselves the possibility that this time our Base Camp staff might be dishonest.

Dawa, who was reputed to be a very capable and experienced Sherpa, arrived with the remaining loads. He resembled, with his tanned complexion, reflective sunglasses, gleaming smile and elegant clothes, a continental ski-instructor rather than a rugged man of the hills. His English was perfect. None of the missing equipment was to be found in the loads he had brought. On the contrary, more that should have been in those loads was missing.

Alan had already had a confrontation with Dawa at the very beginning when he had obviously postponed the start of the walk in for a day on the pretext of there being a hold-up with the porters. Alan had discovered that the real reason was that Dawa had wanted to spend an extra day in the company of an American girl whom he had met whilst leading a trek.

It was odious for us, amidst the raw beauty of the mountains, to have to deal with corruption which we had thought to have left behind. The Sirdar is responsible for the safe transport of the loads of his expedition. There is quite a degree of latitude in this, especially at the end of an expedition when much of the equipment is sold off cheaply or abandoned, but too much of our equipment was missing to let the matter drop.

Dawa refused to accept responsibility for any losses and insisted that everything had arrived. There was an atmosphere of discontent at Base Camp. Much energy seemed to be used up in arguments with the most sullen and uncooperative group of Sherpas I had known. The food we were eating had deteriorated from the wonderful dishes the cook was known to be capable of. There were plenty of tins of food we had brought out from Britain, but these never appeared, and our meals were a tedious affair of rice and dahl (spiced lentils). John was furious when he walked into the kitchen tent to find Dawa consuming a full tin of ham himself His explanation was that he was testing it to see whether it was suitable for himself and the rest of the Base Camp staff. At our insistence on having more than rice and dahl ourselves, the tinned food subsequently appeared on the table – the tin having been heated to thaw out the contents and placed unopened on the table with a tin opener. The cook explained this by saying that he did not know how to handle tinned foods.

It transpired that it was this same Dawa who had sown the seeds of doubt about whether Messner and Habeler had really climbed Everest without oxygen in 1978 and had gone on subsequently to accuse Messner of having stolen treasures from Nepalese monasteries some years previously. We were all uneasy about the situation; Alan felt very much the responsibility of making a decision on this. It was not a step he wanted to take lightly. If he were to dismiss Dawa it would be a serious blow to his career as a Sherpa and so far we had heard nothing but good reports on his capabilities.

Alan decided to let things stand for the moment but Base Camp was not a place I felt comfortable in with all this discord.

Undoubtedly we had been disappointed to learn that a Japanese expedition was to attempt to climb the mountain at the same time as us. Their objective was to be on the opposite side of the mountain, climbing by the South Col route, the way by which the mountain has been climbed many times before. We knew little about their expedition until we reached Base Camp, having heard that it was an attempt at a solo ascent by Naomi Uemura. At thirty-nine, Uemura is the most famous of Japanese mountaineers and amongst other things had completed a solo crossing of the North Pole. At first it had hardly impinged on us that anyone else would be on the mountain. We imagined that Uemura's solo ascent would involve him and possibly a couple of Sherpas as Base Camp staff. Everest seemed big enough to accommodate him as well as us. It was a complete surprise on arrival, therefore, to find that there were dozens of Japanese climbers, journalists and television people occupied with this much vaunted 'solo' ascent. They also had an even larger number of Sherpas equipped to work on the mountain.

We would rather have had the mountain to ourselves but as it was we would only come into contact with the Japanese at Base Camp. Their route would take them off at right angles to the direction we were going. They would have to climb up the tumbling chaos of the Khumbu Icefall into the snowy valley of the Western Cwm. There they had to traverse beneath the South West Face of the mountain to reach the opposite side to where we would be climbing. From our precarious vantage points on the way up to the Lho La, we could sometimes see the minute dots of the Japanese or their Sherpas picking their way through the maze of crevasses and toppling blocks in the icefall, as they went round to the south side of the mountain. Paradoxically, though their route is the easiest way up, gaining it entails crossing the most dangerous area of the mountain.

The Japanese were neighbours, camped only a few hundred yards away. Alan went over to pay a courtesy call. He came back with an invitation for all of us to go across in the evening for a meal. It promised to be a welcome change from rice and dahl.

The Japanese tents were in a slight hollow, not completely visible from our camping place. From above a swelling in the surface of the glacier could be seen the many pinnacles of their orange tents. It looked to be an enormous camp. Towards evening, well insulated for a short journey, we trooped across in the direction of their lights.

On closer acquaintance the many pinnacles appeared to be clustered closely together; my perception could not resolve what I was seeing. A large tent flap opened, spilling electric light out on to the ice, and we stumbled inside after each other, blinded by the unexpected brightness. We were inside a huge marquee. The pinnacles were not closely grouped tents after all, but one enormous tent with many points, the like of which I had never seen before. Outside an electric generator throbbed away and a string of glowing bulbs ran the whole length of this grandiose construction. The chimney of a wood-burning stove disappeared upwards to be lost in the voluminous folds of the tent's inner lining, and a long, low, narrow table ran the length of the room with armchairs made from bamboo cane on either side of it.

Sometimes I have the sensation that I am no longer contributing to events, but am being controlled by them as they happen. I couldn't grasp what was happening – Everest, winter, cold and discomfort and suddenly we were in a cocoon of luxury, surrounded by smiling faces, flashing, whirring cameras and microphones, warm and comfortable. Some small plastic bottles were produced from a box and Naomi Uemura, grinning broadly, said: 'This is Saki. We bring to celebrate our summit climb. But now we celebrate you coming.'

We all drank and sat and grinned. More details of this unbelievable tent registered in my mind. I did not like to stare – I felt as if I was in someone's private rooms. Along each wall was a row of curtained alcoves perhaps six feet long by four feet wide. These were the sleeping places for the Japanese members, with a thin partition of nylon as a concession to privacy. At the furthest end of the tent was a bank of electrical consoles. 'Is that a hi-fi system?' one of our team asked hopefully. 'No, it is a facsimile machine for weather reports from Delhi.'

The cost of transporting all of this equipment must have been enormous. Only the name of Uemura had made it possible as the expedition was backed by a Japanese TV company and newspaper.

I was interested to meet Uemura. The chubby-faced, boyish looks gave no suggestion of the man's acknowledged hardiness, nor of the determination which had driven him during the many months of his solo Arctic crossing.

'How is Don Whillan? Is he still climbing?' Uemura had spent much time with Don on Everest's South West Face in 1971.

He seemed at ease, with a youthful enjoyment of drinking and joking. It was not the hardship he must have put up with in the Arctic crossing but the deadly boredom of months of solitude which I found amazing.

'Are you married? What does your wife think of you spending so much time away?'

'My wife is very happy for me.'

The Japanese were interested in our ages. Uemura felt, at thirty-nine, that he was coming to the end of his active years.

His expedition also had a scientific project, with three scientists taking bore samples from the glacier and sending them back to Kathmandu. Two doctors, a journalist and a film crew completed the team. Uemura had spent some weeks in the region during the winter of 1979/80 and had realised the importance of having a comfortable Base Camp. For this reason he had returned to Japan where he had two purpose-built tents made to withstand the wind and cold.

Further down the table other members of our team were having different conversations. There were a number of other Japanese climbers on the expedition, one of whom said: 'I have contract to go to 200 metres from summit. After that only Mr Uemura goes alone.'

Someone was talking to the Sirdar of the Japanese Sherpas: 'The British expedition will reach top of mountain before Japanese, because Japanese use Sherpas who want money and so make expedition last longer.'

We had stumbled into the tent blinded by the light, now we stumbled out, drunk from the unaccustomed quantities of alcohol, thanking our hosts profusely. Course after course of strange delicacies had appeared before us, most of which I found myself picking at and discreetly leaving to one side. I noticed most of our team doing the same. Our digestive systems had still scarcely adjusted to the altitude and the food we were more familiar with; to have forced down exotic morsels, with to us a bizarre taste, would have invited disaster. I hoped that we had not caused mortal offence in terms of the Japanese code of conduct, but there was no way to tell from their excessive demonstrations of politeness and goodwill.

Back at our own camp we separated each to his own tent.

The Japanese set-up was certainly a contrast. As I slid, fully dressed, into my sleeping bag, the thermometer read -11 degrees Celsius!

On Tuesday 9 December John Porter joined the Burgess twins and myself in going back up towards the Lho La. There were still many jobs to do round Base Camp and four was quite enough at one time to be working on the route. It also gave those who had been struck down with dysentery a chance to regain their strength.

More familiar this time with the way, we lost no time in reaching the high point of the previous day. Al, moving powerfully on ahead, skirted below a wall of rock and traversed back above it. John and I were below as he crossed a slope of loose stones, sending showers of them down on to us. I was out of line of fire, but John was caught in the open, cursing loudly as the stones bounced off his helmet. Al stopped moving as we shouted abuse at him and stayed motionless and looking apologetically sheepish until we had caught him up. We did not let ourselves get separated again.

We had brought a rucksack each full of rope to fix in place on the more difficult ground. We would have to go up and down many times before we were finished with the mountain, so to save time and ensure safety we had brought rope to leave as a handline where it was necessary, once we had climbed a section. On the biggest mountains it is hardly possible to climb continuously upwards day after day. A period of acclimatisation is essential. We did not have a fully predetermined plan about how to climb the mountain, but we were finding that the best method was to fix rope on the difficult ground. Sometimes we only climbed a few hundred feet a day, but with rope once fixed in place, ascent was much more rapid. To have placed a camp after only a few hundred feet would have been futile and would have necessitated carrying enormous weights of tentage, food and equipment. By linking together the efforts of each day to place a camp only after a major section was completed, we gave ourselves a chance of acclimatising in the process and made a more economical use of our resources.

An area of grey, granite slabs stretched up out of the evil looking gully at which we had stopped the day before. I stayed back filming the other three as they scurried across the broken, rocky bed of the gully to a promontory on the far side. Being in the bottom of the gully held the sensation of being in the bottom of a rubbish chute, a focal point for anything thrown from above. The gully was an alien place. We felt much more at ease on the smooth, grey slabs above.

These were not difficult, but it would save time, when carrying a heavy load, to have a rope in place, and if it should snow heavily there were other places where we might need fixed ropes.

It had been another clear, fine day when we had left. Rapidly it had changed; the ambient air temperature was always well below freezing point, and it was only the heat of the sun which gave the impression that a day was warm. Once the sun was masked by cloud, or a wind started, the bitterness of winter made itself felt. By the time we had reached the grey slabs we were cold. For once the Burgess twins, usually so careful, were caught unawares, and as soon as they had used up the rope out of their sacks they rushed off down to avoid the danger of exposure.

John and I, better clothed, were able to continue. John felt guilti-ly responsible for the weather. The Sherpas had caught him burn-ing some rubbish at Base Camp that morning and had given him a ticking off. They had said it was bad to burn rubbish as it brought bad weather. John viewed his handiwork with a resigned air. None of us is really superstitious but on a mountain, when in a state of nervous tension, one can be susceptible to anything that is said or held with conviction. On Kangchenjunga we had not walked the last ten feet to the summit as the people of Sikkim believe this would desecrate the home place of the gods they believe live there and cause them to send floods and earthquakes in revenge. We did not see any gods and did not hold these beliefs, but an ominous storm was approaching the mountain and a huge black bird hung over the summit watching us. No word had passed, but none of us thought to trespass further.

John has a slight, stooping build, belying a tough resilience. As I got to know him I realised that his quietness was reflective. He was what I would consider to be an intellectual, nurturing his knowledge and reproducing it at the most apt moments. He has an apologetic manner which conceals the strengths which moti-vate him, and which earned him the respect of the Poles with whom he had taken to climbing after a visit to Poland as part of an official exchange group of mountaineers.

As he descended a precarious ramp into yet another horrifying gully I was glad that he seemed unperturbed at the prospect before us. This gully was steeper, encircled at the top by a basin of convolut-ed ice. How steep it was, was hard to judge, and secretly, with the cowardliness of innermost thoughts, I hoped that John would have enough rope to get the measure of the difficulties before I took over.

He climbed along the edge of the gully, up on to the ice as far as he could go. I joined him and he led off again, this time forced into the bed of the gully, a runnel with dirty smears on the ice where rocks had struck on their way down. More loose blocks were balanced one on top of another and John eased his way past them, his legs spread wide across the narrowed funnel of rock which reared up out of the top rim of the ice. He went out of sight, the rope still moving slowly upwards, then came the sound of the hammering of pitons into rock and a shout for me to come.

It was my turn to go first. I had to cross the gully and climb the opposite wall of ice to an overhanging rock groove which appeared to end on the crest of the ridge and at the Lho La. The ice still looked steep, even from close to, and I felt nervous.

A thirty-foot-high step of rock blocked the way to the ice; it required some delicate moves, awkward in the huge, clumsy boots I was wearing. I felt the surge of nervous excitement as I moved tentatively upwards on small footholds to where I could place a piton and achieve some security. The ice was steep but it was pockmarked with weather-worn holes into which I could step, and a few projecting rocks frozen into place provided the infrequent handhold. As usual the encounter was not as frightening as the anticipation. I reached the bottom of the rock wall running into the overhanging groove and secured the rope.

Above I could see signs of the Yugoslav expedition – the remnants of a wire ladder and frayed ropes. The 300-foot groove above clearly presented considerable difficulties. It was late in the afternoon, we had used all our rope and I turned to descend.

The following day Paul, Brian and Pete, carrying heavy loads of rope, went up to make a cache of equipment ready for the major assault on the groove and the anticipated breakthrough on to the Lho La. They were now recovered from the illness, having only coughs and sore throats which the cold, dry air continued to irritate. Alan had been hit worst by the dysentery and was fighting hard to shake off the sickness which was sapping his strength. He busied himself at Base Camp with calculations of the expedition's finances, food and fuel consumption and general estimations of our progress. The sickness was going right through the camp; Ade was next taken ill.

Five of us went up next; Al and John fastened themselves into the overhanging groove preparing for a long siege. Brian and Pete laboured up with more loads, signalling their movements with periodic bursts of noisy coughing. I lodged myself on to a ledge on the opposite side of the gully with a movie camera and watched Al's distant, matchstick moves up the yellow rock.

The remains of the wire ladder hung temptingly down the groove, but the wire was frayed and the rungs bent and twisted either from rockfall or winds. I could see Al testing it and hesitatingly groping his way upwards on the rock with grunts and pauses for breath, preferring to climb the rock which he could rely on than trust to an abandoned hawser. His muffled exchanges with John belaying him carried across the gully; it was clear that he was having a struggle.

Some rock broke away from under his foot and ricocheted across the gully to just below where I was sitting. John looked over to me. Neither of us said anything; there was nothing to say.

The groove and the wall up which Al was finding the way, was exceptionally difficult climbing for the altitude. It looked as if it might be technically the most interesting climbing on the route. We would not be able to cope with anything as difficult as this higher up the mountain, as the ever more rarefied air would not sustain the strenuous efforts required. I was partly envious and partly relieved that someone else was leading this section. I would have liked the satisfaction of solving this particularly difficult problem first, but there were other essential roles to play; I was filming the ascent for ITN; Brian and Pete were carrying loads in support, possibly the most tedious and unrecognised contribution to any expedition. Given that with honour I could sit back, I did feel a guilty self-indulgence at watching someone else struggling to force a way up the rock and fix rope in place for everyone else to follow.

The gully was deep and caught the heat of the sun. The wind did not penetrate but could be heard whistling over the top of the ridge, a few hundred feet above. The heat of the sun loosened some rocks; with increasing frequency stones began to fall past my eyrie. Had the stones been falling when I had arrived there I would not have stayed but I had been there half an hour before the first fell and had come to feel at home. It was slow progress up the groove; I did not want to miss filming the last moments as Al moved up on to the ridge, and I sat for three hours, pressing myself hard against the rock behind me to avoid the stones which by the end were falling every ten minutes. Once Al knocked down a massive block which shattered on impact and sprayed all around me. John looked helplessly on.

Al reached a ledge at half height and John climbed up the rope to join him, using jumar clamps which slide up the rope and locked, taking most of the difficulty out of the ascent. The second half of the wall went more quickly and a jubilant Al shouted down that he had reached a platform, but not the Lho La.

I was as relieved as he was; I could quit the perch in the firing range and ferry my load up to the top of the ropes Al had fixed in place. It was indeed an impressive performance by Al, as I realised on reaching the groove. The first bit was overhanging and, even with the ropes, very strenuous. It took me an hour to climb the wall and join John and Al. Pete and Brian appeared in the gully below and I warned them to stay clear on account of the falling stones.

Enough had been achieved for the day. Short of energy and time we returned to Base Camp. Psychologically it was very good to have overcome such a major obstacle, though further difficult ground barred the way to the plateau. If the whole route continued as hard and slow as this section it boded ill for our chances.

We sat in our dining tent discussing tactics and experiences. The tent was shabby and cold by comparison with the Japanese pavilion. We had one small paraffin stove on the table to give a semblance of heat, but it was necessary to wear padded clothing even inside. Huddled together round the yellow light of a paraffin lamp we resembled the scenes I had seen in photographs of Shackleton's men in their winter hut. This was the norm for our existence now – spells of hard work interspersed with periods of inactivity occupied in formless discussion of strategy and often drifting into another exchange of yarns from the past.

Al, still buzzing with the thrill of the hard climbing he had done, told us one tale in which he outlined a patent technique from his teaching days for keeping his class, in a rather rough school, quiet: 'I used to play loud music on the hi-fi I'd fitted up in the class – Jimi Hendrix or Frank Zappa – have it on really loud so they couldn't hear themselves talk, so they had to work and anyway they were used to the constant noise at home of the TV so it was better for them to work with noise.' All this was recounted with a constant flexing of the shoulders and a devilish grin on his face.

More loads were carried up next day but harrowing winds drove everyone back down without further progress being made. In the middle of the night I was half aware of the noise of the wind and of people's voices and footsteps. In the morning our camp was a shambles. Three tents were collapsed, their poles broken, and others were badly awry. An enormous plume of cloud spewed horizontally north from the summit of Nuptse.

The previous day one of the visiting party of Japanese, admiring our down suits, oxtail soup and route up to the Lho La, had pointed at a motionless wind generator, which had not so far produced any electricity – 'I hope it never works.' It was now spinning furiously.

The whole day was taken up with patching tents, reinforcing tent poles and building crude walls, from the rocks littering the ice, as wind-breaks round the tents.

Dawa and the rest of the Base Camp staff stood, watching our exertions, without the slightest offer of help. Feelings against Dawa had become even more antipathetic since Alan, in going through the accounts, had discovered that Dawa had spent three times as much bringing the loads he was in charge of to Base Camp than Alan himself had. Seven thousand rupees more than expected had been spent. Dawa explained this away by saying he had had to pay more for porters as they were unwilling to carry in winter and one porter had fallen and broken his leg, for which he had had to pay for hospitalisation. It was a plausible, but unsatisfactory explanation.

The arrival of our mail runner the next day brought a welcome bundle of mail, but also a letter from our expedition agent in Kathmandu, through whom we had hired our Sherpas. Alan had written to him about earlier difficulties with Dawa, and in his reply our agent said that if we did have difficulties we should go ahead and dismiss him. An enclosed copy of a letter direct to Dawa from the agent emphasised his displeasure at the reported conduct, and mentioned this as casting further bad light on his behaviour after the incident with the Numbur expedition the previous year, an occasion when much valuable equipment from a Norwegian expedition had mysteriously disappeared.

On being questioned, Dawa launched into a diatribe against the affluent expedition members who employ Sherpas who do not want to work for them but who want the money and have no alternative.

There was mention in the letter from the agent of Dawa's expressed intention to leave us, as soon as we reached Base Camp, to go to America with the girl who had caused him to delay the start of the approach march. There were too many damning coincidences and too much suspicion on our part for us to let the matter go any further. After much agonised soul-searching, Alan went to speak to our Liaison Officer and explain to him that we wanted to dismiss Dawa.

Mr Singh, the Liaison Officer, was the representative of the government of Nepal and it was through him that any complaint and request for action had to be formally made. He was a small, shy man who rarely entered into conversation unless spoken to and spent much of his time performing a self-imposed routine of exercises and singing Hindu songs. However, when confronted with the unpleasant task of executing the wishes of the team, he did not demur. He readily grasped the issues involved and concurred with the conclusions reached. Dawa was summoned and formally dismissed.

It was a sad episode which seemed totally at odds with the spirit of the expedition, but with Dawa's departure, though brought about with pain, came welcome relief, much as the removal of an aching tooth.

Alan was deeply affected by the incident and the events leading up to it. He had been one of the most explicit exponents of the concept of our expedition as leaderless. I had spent some time with him prior to our departure, making frequent journeys to London during which we discussed the rationale behind the expedition. He firmly believed that all of us were sufficiently experienced not to need a leader in the traditional sense of having an overall director of affairs. In fact he felt such a system would be counter-productive in that it could easily engender antagonism amongst a group of highly individualistic human beings. However, he accepted the title of 'leader' as being necessary in dealing with sponsors and the media in Britain, who found it impossible to cope with the concept of a 'leaderless expedition', and with the Nepalese government, who insist on having someone nominated as leader.

It thus fell to Alan to express the decision of the group and no matter what his philosophy of democracy was, the very fact of being spokesman seemed to cause him to be more deeply affected by the responsibility of having to express a group decision than his own part in that decision warranted.

Alan's training as a mathematician led him to delight in intricate discussions involving logic and hypothetical musings which went over most of our heads. He has something of the sophist in him, taking the opposite side in an argument for the sake of prolonging a debate, and he did this in the discussions over Dawa in order to ensure that we erred on the side of mercy rather than acted too quickly and unjustly, until it became clear that a source of continuous discord would not be removed until Dawa was dismissed.

Even democrat leadership brings the loneliness of decision-making, but a cheering indicator that this decision had been the right one came as soon as Dawa left. The rest of the Base Camp staff, who had been a sullen and uncooperative group after the arrival of the Sirdar, were transformed immediately he left. They could be heard singing and chatting as we had not noticed them doing for a few days, and there was a new mood of cooperation and willingness to help.

5 THE LHO LA

For two days the weather had remained calm and clear. Expecting the worst, we tended to be suspicious of our good fortune, believing that we had not seen the real face of winter yet, for otherwise, apart from the short days and bitter nights, this would be an ideal season for climbing compared with the unstable spells before and after the monsoon. As it was, lower peaks, not so affected by the jet-stream winds and requiring shorter time for their ascent, could well be climbed in these clear December days.

Alan Rouse was feeling physically much better as well as psychologically relieved that the incident with Dawa was now over, and he went up with the Burgess twins and John Porter. In spite of it being his first time out from Base Camp, Alan was able to reach the top of the overhanging groove and spent all day with John tediously hauling loads up from below. It was too exhausting to climb the fixed ropes and the now repaired wire ladder with a full sack on one's back. Climbing the corner consumed time and energy, so whilst the twins found the way and fixed rope along the ridge above the corner, Alan and John formed a stock pile of equipment.

The rest of the ridge was unexpectedly hard. Behind the yellow wall of rock, up which ropes had been painstakingly fastened, was a vast amphitheatre 200 feet wide separating the top of the wall from the Lho La plateau. It plunged in 2,000 feet of avalanche-scoured rock and ice to the glacier. Blocks of ice stood, like rows of houses, waiting their turn, and the loss of equilibrium as the mother bed of ice advanced, to plunge and shatter into a million pieces to form another immense avalanche. If hell were a cold place its entrance would resemble this.

To reach the Lho La the twins had to climb in a rising arc along the ridge of rock which encircled the top of the amphitheatre. Much of the way was easy, with short steps of vicious difficulty, overcome with much exertion and panting. The very atmosphere of the place was enough to inspire nervousness, but the rock itself had also become massively loose. The final hundred feet horizontally rightwards to gain the snow was on blocks adhering, without visible support, to the wall behind. 'The traverse of the eggshells' became its name. On reaching the snow, out of rope and ready to descend, Alan was disappointed to find still no sign of a place in which to pitch a tent or dig a cave.

At Base Camp Paul, Brian and myself made ready to go up the next day with every intention of establishing a tent or snow cave, in order to stay on the mountain. The film team had been strangely inactive for a while; I began to wonder if they were being affected by the altitude and slipping into a routine which made it seem as if there was not enough time to do everything, but proved a tendency to put off doing anything until another occasion. Many expedition films fail to succeed entirely on account of this – just surviving on a daily basis at Base Camp can be quite exhausting enough. Allen Jewhurst, director of the film, however, had gone up to the start of the fixed ropes in the company of the lead party, to weigh up camera positions. Unfamiliar with the route, he had sat and waited till Paul, who was making a short carry with a load to the start of the fixed ropes, arrived and descended with him.

It was dusk when John, looking worn and weary, burst into the dining tent where the rest of us were settling into our places for the evening. A growing anxiety at the late return of everyone from the hill was immediately relieved. John sank down on to a box for a seat and questions about the day's climbing started. John has a way of not answering questions immediately nor in the way expected.

'The others aren't going to get here before dark, I don't think they've got torches and they are short of a pair of crampons.'

Everyone looked at him; they were not the words expected in answer to the questions. My mind ran over a checklist of essentials and their whereabouts – ice axe, crampons, torch, spare torch, mitts, boots. Brian next to me seemed to be doing the same. John took the silence for reluctance to stir out into the cold night: 'Look, those guys have been working hard all day and are struggling down in the dark. Are you going to sit here on your arses? They need torches to get across the glacier. I'd go back but I'm knackered.'

It was a startling outburst. John, fully dressed for the cold outside, still with his crampons on, did not realise that anyone going out into the night would have to get ready. It might take ten minutes, it might take two hours to locate and return with the other three, but to venture out unprepared invited disaster. Bare hands would be numb in minutes.

Brian and I scratched around in the dark inside and outside our tents, trying to remember where things were, and, prepared as best we could, hurried urgently over uneven ground towards the slopes up the Lho La. The night was still but there was no sound carried on the air; tragedy in the mountains can occur from the most innocuous situation, and flutterings of unease tightened my stomach. Where the ice was no longer roughened by rubble we stopped and strapped crampons to our boots to allow us, to walk more easily on the undulating, glistening surface. We followed the pools of light cast by our torches along the marks on the ice made by the earlier passage of our feet and then, unheralded, the chattering voices of swaying figures rose up from out of a hollow to meet us. There was laughter and ribald curses from the trio, making me feel foolish for the anxiety I had felt for them.

They were tired and indeed had no torch; Alan and Al were sharing a pair of crampons – one boot each securely bound with a row of metal spikes to give purchase on the ice, the other, rubber-soled, slipping and unbalancing their gait, making a mockery of any pretensions to be experienced mountaineers.

There was a warm comradeship in our meeting.

'Thanks for coming to meet us, lads,' said Ade, 'it's really been hard work getting across in the dark.'

We returned together to camp, seeing the dining tent now as a cosy haven by comparison with the outside world.

I awoke from a disturbing dream in which I was hanging by the neck and a vision of failure on the route. There were no grounds for these unsettling dreams except that I had gone to sleep with a familiar feeling of apprehension before embarking on the next stage of the climb, the next step into the unknown.

Movement and a sense of fitness banished such chimeras in the bright light of day. I reached the top of the fixed ropes by 1.30pm., weighed down by a sack which held, in addition to the essentials for a stay of two or three nights, 40 pounds of food and gear. Paul and Brian, similarly laden, were also toiling up the ropes to stay.

We planned to start digging a snow cave and, if this was not big enough to sleep in by evening, to erect a tent for the night. We had little hope of a tent lasting very long in the winds of the Lho La, but hoped to dispense with it after one night. There was nowhere in sight that seemed suitable to start digging a cave. Hard, icy snow swept upwards at too precarious an angle for siting a cave. Rationalising the situation, I knew that we would not do any digging at all this day, there was still some gear to be picked up from the cache at the top of the corner and there was not even a place where we could put up a tent.

Dumping my sack, I scrambled upwards on easier ground, kicking the edge of my boot into the snow and holding on to the rock against which it abutted. It was a foolish but delightful romp, liberated from the weight of my sack and the constriction of being fastened into a rope. I would not be allowed even one slip, not one error of judgement, but I had the strength and confidence of fitness, reaching up and testing each handhold before pulling up on it; kicking a boot into the snow and trying my weight on that foot before committing myself to it completely. The enthusiasm was rewarded; a broad ledge, ten feet wide, opened up to my left. It was littered with rocks, easily wide enough for a tent and the rocks could be made into a wall as a wind-break. Reassured at this alternative to a frantic attempt at excavating a snow cave as a shelter for the night, I turned to descend and propose the change of plan to Paul and Brian.

I had not looked down as I climbed upwards above the ropes.

As I turned now and saw the ice runnel up which I had come, ending abruptly at the edge of the precipice of the amphitheatre, I felt sick and nervous at the insecurity of my position. I descended the 200 feet back to the ropes with my stomach knotted in apprehension, clutching more tightly than was warranted to every hold, inescapably aware of the folly of my situation.

Paul had reached the end of the ropes when I arrived back. He agreed that it would be most sensible to pitch a tent immediately than risk having no shelter ready by nightfall.

'Did you pick the tent up? I couldn't find it.'

'No, I looked in one of the sacks halfway up the corner, it wasn't in there.'

'Damn, I wonder if Brian's got it.'

'What's it like up to the ledge?'

'O.K., but be careful. You'll be safer with crampons on.'

I slid down the ropes strung along the rim of the amphitheatre and regained the top of the corner with a pleasurable ease which made ridiculous the effort needed to climb upwards on the same ground. I could hear Brian long before I could see him, as his hacking coughs echoed up the corner.

There was no tent with the gear at the top of the corner and Brian didn't have it either. I slid down the ropes of the corner, imagining an ignominious retreat if there was no tent to be found and dreading the long haul back up the ropes if there was.

The tent was concealed in a sack which Paul had not examined; I shouldered the sack and started back up.

The preliminary plan of digging a snow cave for the night had been absurdly ambitious; we had barely time to erect the tent, build a protective wall of rocks and gather snow to melt for the evening meal before sunset and the rapid night took over.

Brian was weary from the journey up. He sank into the dark interior of the tent, thrusting out a grateful hand for mugs of liquid and plates of food as they were prepared. Sometimes his pained face would appear in the light of the stove as he strained forward, shaken by another spasm of coughing.

Heavy-boned and big-framed, Brian gave me, as I grew to know him, the impression that he was always pushing himself hard. If it was recounting lurid stories, Brian strove to produce the most startling; if it was outrageous behaviour, Brian would out-gross anyone. On the mountain I could see him driving himself on against the affliction of his crippling cough long after I would have let myself turn back. Brian was continually forcing himself along the road of excess in his search for the palace of wisdom. I imagined his throat to be raw and bleeding.

Again the night was suspiciously calm. I was numb when I crawled back from the edge of the platform from where I had been futilely attempting to make a radio call to Base Camp thousands of feet below, but only the lightest breeze rocked the tent. Our platform was awesomely poised on the very brink of a precipice, but somehow tucked away from the wind streaming across the Lho La plateau. We spent a restless night, the three of us pressed close together, suffocated with the tent door closed and chilled with it open. Next day I had a headache and the three of us were slow to make a start.

To find a more level area of snow in which we could dig a cave without risk of slipping down a steep slope as soon as one stepped outside, we headed for the plateau of the Lho La itself. A basin of firm snow, split by a number of crevasses, gave way to easier angled slopes that descended to level ground. I was ready to go and Paul suggested I lead off, fixing rope on to aluminium stakes driven into the snow until I was no longer above the gulf of the amphitheatre. There was no advantage to the climbing in having a rope there, but we would have to cross and recross this slope many times, and it would be so much safer with a hand rail in place. Without a fixed rope, a gust of wind could overbalance someone and throw him down the slope into the amphitheatre.

I was nervous of starting off, the slope of snow looked steep, but it was an optical illusion, the yawning abyss a hundred feet below influencing my view of the situation. When I was clear of the abyss, I drove a final stake into the snow and shouted to Paul and Brian to follow.

The snow slope I was on eased down for 300 feet into a level plateau; this in turn swept northwards and down, losing itself in a jagged maze of ice pinnacles; remote, mysterious Tibet lay brown in the distance. Across the plateau rose the icy escarpment of the West Ridge, 3,500 feet of snow, rock and ice to the rounded dome of the shoulder. Lurking elusively, a thrilling sight behind the Western Shoulder, was the summit – so far away. A banner of cloud streamed off it, the symbol of winter, barren and windy. That was our objective but, as usual, I found myself shelving any thought of what was to come and concentrated on the task of the moment.

Brian had spent the summer in the Karakoram at the other end of the Himalayas taking part in the ski descent of Baltoro Kangri. He was enthusiastic about a snow cave they had dug there which, according to the description, sounded like a palace. Paul and I, professing less experience in such matters, looked to Brian for suggestions as to the best place, and method of construction.

There was a science to it; an optimum angle of slope; a method of achieving the correct lengths of entry into the slope before starting to form a chamber. It was hard work, there was no science about that. We were at 20,000 feet and the maximum spell of digging that any of us could do was ten to fifteen minutes. We took it in turns.

John and Ade arrived in the course of the day while Brian and Paul were digging and I was having a rest. 'You're foreman, are you?' Ade joked when he came, watching shovels full of snow being ejected from the hole.

They brought news of Pete injecting the cook boy with an anti-nausea drug; the sickness seemed to be circulating round the camp. Alan was ill again and Al had gone down with the same thing. Usually on an expedition all germs seem to disappear. It is so cold that they are killed off or rendered inactive.

This time, however, in spite of the cold, we seemed to be afflicted by a particularly virulent strain, and once the sickness took hold, recovery was very much harder.

John and Ade did not stay long. They dumped their loads and hurried down. By 4 p.m. we had dug out a cave, big enough for one person. The snow was hard, ideal for climbing, taking only the front points of the crampons to give a secure foothold, but tiresome for digging. The early stages were the worst as the entrance had to be a narrow tunnel to keep out as much wind as possible, which meant that only one of us could work, sometimes on knees, sometimes lying flat, working away under showers of ice splinters. It did not look much for a day's work but there was room now for two people kneeling upright to dig all the time, and next day we expected progress to be much quicker with a habitable snow cave by the time we finished.

Somehow I was manoeuvred into being cook again, a laborious task with much of the time being taken up just melting snow to get the liquid to make a meal or a drink. From start to finish, in order to obtain the necessary bodily intake of fluid, cooking a meal can take three or more hours. I kept dozing off whilst waiting for the snow to melt and the water to boil. The boiling point of water at high altitude is much lower than at sea level. Due to the decreased air pressure, the water, vaporises at a lower temperature, but the heat is not there to cook the food. Most things take three times as long to cook as at sea level.

'Does one of you two want to have a go?'

'You seem better acclimatised than us – we need the rest!'

I realised how Dick Renshaw must have felt on K2 when Pete and I had languished in our sleeping bags whilst he, uninfluenced by any mood of lethargy, used to be up first thing preparing breakfast to get us moving. There is some mechanism of passive resistance on expeditions which conspires to instil a reluctance to make more effort than absolutely necessary, so that making a cup of tea can come to seem like a monstrous task. Yet more than on any other expedition the dehydration effect of altitude and cold was making it essential to drink more than the accepted minimum of eight pints a day and to force oneself to eat whether one felt like it or not. Without the liquid, altitude sickness and headaches occur much more readily, and without the food we would be weak and much more susceptible to the cold.

After another fitful night we worked on the snow cave until the middle of the afternoon. We were weary now and my fatigued muscles seemed to be contributing little to the enlargement of the cave. Al arrived and I followed him down to Base Camp, having dismantled the tent lest it should be blown away by the wind. Paul and Brian followed later. There was the warm ache of tiredness in my legs as I crossed the glacier back to camp and the thicker air of Base Camp made me drowsy. Alan, worn out by his debilitating sickness, looked jaded and depressed.

We now had a base for action on the West Ridge itself. The ascent up to the Lho La had been technically much more difficult than we had expected, and more difficult than anything else we hoped to find higher up. It felt to me like a preparation, an essential and unavoidable part of the climb, but nonetheless only a preparation, and that it was from the Lho La that I would begin to feel that real progress was being made. For the three of us who had been up there it was time for a rest but I envied the discoveries that those who were going up next would make as they explored new ground.

6 PROGRESS AND PUNISHMENT

The mail runner arrived while we were on the mountain. With the welcome letters was the surprise of a newspaper, *The Observer*, three weeks late but a prized arrival all the same, complete with colour supplement. We were sending back news reports to *The Observer* and they had agreed to mail to us a copy each week during the expedition. I spent a whole day leisurely soaking up every bit of world news, cinema critiques, book reviews and even business news. It mattered little that it was all three weeks out of date.

Our shy little Liaison Officer, glued to his radio for much of the day, sometimes volunteered a snippet of news, or the Japanese passed on something they had picked up on their radio. It was thus we came to learn of, and be shocked unaccountably by John Lennon's death. There was a strange sense of *déjà vu* in this two-stage arrival of news. One associates newspapers with almost the same instantaneous transmission of news as the radio or television. For us the time-lag between the two was so great that the news from the radio had passed into the subconscious long before the paper arrived, so that I read *The Observer* with an uncanny and mistaken sensation of prescience.

There was no organised manner in which we went up on the mountain. In keeping with the democratic ideals of the expedition it was held that everyone was capable enough and experienced enough to make decisions themselves on the mountain; everyone was mature enough to work to his maximum and consequently there was no need for any direction of effort. Thus there was no order in which anyone went up to carry loads or occupy the snow cave or push the route further. Not everyone was in agreement over this. The Burgess twins were vociferous in their condemnation of what they called 'random attack'; John believed that everyone should do a certain number of trips just carrying loads up to the Lho La before moving up. Alan was adamant that everyone was working to his limit and that no more could be expected: 'There may be an uneven distribution of what is being done at the moment, but by the end of the trip it will all have balanced out.' Nevertheless, there was feeling in some quarters that more organisation and coordination would not be a bad thing.

The Burgess twins, John and Pete moved up to occupy and enlarge the snow cave. Two of them stayed in the tent for a night until a second adjoining cave was dug, making ample space for all eight of us. They made the mistake of leaving the tent up on a windy night and on the next day, going to ferry some gear across from it to the caves, found it collapsed. The 'unbreakable' fibreglass poles had been eroded away by the action of the wind shaking the tent incessantly throughout a night and rubbing the poles against a rock used to hold the tent down. Inside the snow cave only the sound of the wind penetrated as a distant drone and it was possible to forget its power and persistence.

At Base Camp, intermittently resting and carrying loads up to the Lho La, I was hard put to decide on the best way of utilising a rest day. The hours of sun were so short and life outside those hours was a misery. The meal times were the focal points of the day, starting with the rattling of pans and kettles in the early morning, signifying the preparation of 'bed tea', the most welcome tradition established by the great pioneers of Himalayan mountaineering. Before the day can start, the ritual of tea being brought round and thrust with a grinning 'Morning, sahib, tea' into the tent has to take place. One feels its absence with an irritation similar to that when the milkman has somehow failed to deliver and a cheerless breakfast with black coffee and no cereal starts the day. It is as if it is a God-given right and impossible to stir from the sleeping bag without it. But once the tea arrives and the whole, hot pint is swallowed, it is not many minutes before there is a series of scufflings and pulling of cords and zips as everyone is forced to rush outside to relieve a full bladder. The worst situation occurs when the bio-rhythms are not properly regulated or a pre-dawn sortie into a chill world is brought on by the Pavlovian rattle of kettles and cups from the cook tent.

The dining tent was the centre of the camp, the place where we socialised, discussed, bragged, argued and ate. I felt isolated in my own tent, but unable to concentrate in the dining tent if I wanted to read and there were conversations going on.

One discussion revolved around tactics on the mountain. Alan was all in favour of using snow caves all the way. He and Brian had been part of a team that had climbed the North Face of Nuptse in 1979 and had been impressed with the use of snow caves there. I believed that he was underestimating the difficulty involved in digging snow caves at altitude and said that we would need a cave for at least six people on the West Shoulder at about 23,000 feet and four people at 25,000 feet. I calculated this on the basis of having a rotation of people on the mountain both for digging the caves in the first place and going to the summit at the end. Unless there was accommodation for at least four people at 25,000 feet there would be a gap of several days between one pair going for the top and the next pair.

The twins descended from the Lho La and discussion turned towards the summit. Faced with the overwhelming reality of Everest in winter, fanciful ideas bandied around in England disappeared and now Al voiced his opinion: 'I think that it's going to need all our efforts to get two people to the top. There's no way we are all going to get there. Two of us getting up will be good enough for me.'

The style of expedition we had all evolved relied not upon a meticulous, computer-planned strategy but more upon experience and the ability to judge, on the spot, how best to utilise our resources. We had no selected summit pair; we all had an equal chance of making an attempt to reach the top. Who it would actually be would depend upon how well anyone was performing at that time. The ideal would be for everyone to make it but the 'wastage rate' on mountains is high and this never happens.

We decided on the number and location of camps or snow caves as we went along, aiming to have, at the end, the facility for at least two people to occupy the final camp at 27,000 feet, in striking distance of the summit. In the next camp down, in our case at 25,000 feet, there would have to be room for the returning summit pair and those moving up to take their place. The next camp down again, needing less effort to establish, could be larger than required to hold the rest of the team, in order to accommodate also anyone returning from above. The camps lower down needed to be large enough to facilitate the establishment of the higher camps, and once this had taken place they would become simply transit points on the way up the mountain.

The work done so far and that which remained to do was staggering. It did not do to think of the mountain – Everest, the biggest mountain in the world – it was best to think only of the next little bit, at most to consider the general direction to the next possible campsite, but in detail only the few feet immediately ahead. My mind quailed if it tried to comprehend the whole, but it could cope with bits at a time.

From the snow caves on the Lho La – Stalingrad as we called them (in memory of the bitter winter campaign of the Second World War around that city) – the occupants had attacked the slopes up to the West Shoulder. The twins and John Porter crossed the hostile moonscape of the Lho La and John described reaching the bergschrund, the crevasse which forms where easier angled ice rears up into the steeper wall of a mountain:

> Overnight the wind had dropped to a gentle gale blowing up from Tibet. We had been late leaving the cave and the shadow cast by the West Shoulder had already receded half the distance across the Lho La, between the cave and the start of the slopes. When we reached the bergschrund, Ade, jangling with the snow stakes and ice screws hanging from his waist, volunteered to lead.
>
> The crevasse separating us by ten feet from the

vertical wall of ice opposite was tenuously bridged by a jumble of perched, interlocking ice blocks from some earlier avalanche. Ade made a frightening hop-scotch over these blocks and picked away at the steep, brittle ice with his axe and hammer, trying to lodge them securely. Al filmed his brother's struggles; time passed slowly and the cold penetrated our down suits.

There was fifteen feet of vertical ice before the angle eased back. Ade tottered upwards, suspended above the pale blue depths of the crevasse by the picks of his ice axe and hammer and the crampon points protruding from the front of his boots. His movements were slow but deliberate and, just as the sunlight streamed round the ridge on to us, he was over the worst and securing himself on the easier ground above.

Al and I, in turn, swung up the rope now fastened in place. The slope stretching upwards was not difficult, firm snow enabling a steady ascent. Much more of a problem was making a secure anchor for the rope which we were fixing in place and leaving to provide a rapid way of descent and re-ascent for the future. We led out each rope length in turns, at the end of which it was necessary to dig a deep trench to find firmer snow into which to drive the three-foot-long aluminium stakes. The rope was fastened to a stake and the other two would come up carrying rucksacks filled with more rope.

The slope was at an aggravating angle, too steep to allow one to relax into automatic movements, and yet not quite steep enough to bring out the full concentration needed on more difficult ground. We were disappointed to realise we had only climbed about 600 feet in all before it was time to return to the snow cave.

At Base we received the news with satisfaction. Radio contact had finally been established by the simple expedient of synchronising our watches, so that both parties were attempting to make contact at the same time! Crackling over the air came Ade's voice. It had been difficult, and particularly cold, crossing the bergschrund and the wall of ice behind. He asked for comments on the line to follow. A thousand feet above the point they had reached, a barrier of overhanging, ice-smattered rock spanned the face. It was difficult from their position on the face to decide on the most suitable place to aim for. Too far to the right would bring them into the fall-line of the ice cliffs which projected threateningly above the barrier. I had considered the problem earlier and suggested making for a groove through the barrier into which a tongue of ice penetrated. Usually, where there is ice or snow, the angle of slope is easier. Vertical rock often sloughs it off.

During a warmer season we might have considered doing without the ropes on some sections, and even considered climbing the mountain in 'alpine style', starting at the bottom and continuing to the top in one journey, rather than fixing ropes in place and descending each night to an established camping place. Neither way is easy. Climbing alpine style means carrying everything one needs for survival on one's back: food, cooking equipment, tent or snow shovel. Too heavy a sack and the chances of reaching the summit are much reduced, for a load of 30 pounds is crippling above 20,000 feet. For us, climbing in winter, we had to have much more warm clothing, food and fuel than in summer and the difficulties of our chosen route were much greater than the routes normally followed on the mountain. Progress would be unconscionably slow and the consequences of being caught out by night and storm would be quick and lethal. Fixing ropes in place gave us a quick descent to a secure camp or cave and a means of more rapid ascent to the high point from where further progress could be made.

Whichever way a big mountain is climbed it is rarely enjoyable; the comparison is really between the tedium of climbing and descending known ground several times, making steady upward progress with only the leading pair receiving the real thrill of discovery and contest with difficulty, and the excruciating punishment of attempting to push on upwards each day without the body having a chance to adjust itself to the altitude. In time the composition of the blood alters, more oxygen can be absorbed, the heart does not need to work so hard, adaptation to cold takes place and one's ability to cope with the abnormal conditions of altitude and low temperatures is increased. Trying to rush upwards before this adaptation occurs can be fatal. The slow, measured ascent, fixing ropes and descending each night to sleep lower than the height reached puts the body to much less risk.

The twins and John made sorties from the cave on to the icy slopes to climb and fasten more ropes to stakes driven into the ice; or to pitons driven into rocks which protruded in places. A rope is 150 feet long, a useful, manageable length. Five rope lengths fixed in place represented a day's work. Stretched out flat on the ground, five rope lengths represents barely 250 yards, which would take a matter of minutes to pass over. The next day, John started leading on the wind-swept ice of the West Ridge:

> We mounted confidently up the ropes we had fixed, and continued upwards with more ropes towards the rock barrier above. The barrier appeared deceptively close but it was 1, 000 feet above the bergschrund before we reached the first slabs of rock leading up to the jutting overhangs. We were faced with a confusing sweep of blank granite up which there seemed to be no way to climb. I led across leftwards, with less optimism, to what looked to be a more feasible line up some ice runnels which cut through the rock towards a narrowing in the overhangs above.
>
> At one point we were unexpectedly immersed in a hissing spindrift avalanche – nothing serious, just a massive bombardment of ice crystals. Ade was thirty feet down to my right, the sun directly behind him, and he came miraculously aglow as the ice

particles bounced into the bright light. A red and blue halo formed around his down suit and sack.

I was dissatisfied with the slowness of our progress, but looking across the Lho La to the distant, dark speck that was the snow cave, I realised the scale of the slopes we were on. I knew that Brian and Pete were waiting in the cave and I anticipated their scepticism about the meagreness of *our* efforts; we had fixed only 400 feet of rope this time. They would appreciate the problems themselves when they took over next day.

The twins and John Porter descended to Base Camp leaving Pete Thexton and Brian Hall to solve the problem of the rock barrier.

Paul Nunn, Alan Rouse, Brian and I had carried on ferrying loads up to the Lho La. There was no point in our moving up yet, and there was no more useful function we could serve than to stock up the Lho La camp (Camp 1), so that when it should be necessary for everyone to stay up there would be plenty of food, fuel and rope.

Brian and Alan decided to go up to stay, to replace two of the others after a couple of days. Alan was struggling against the disability of his racking cough and bouts of nausea, determined not to be left behind on account of any sickness. But on the day they were to stay up, Brian, leading up the slabs into the top gully, dislodged a rock that fell and gashed Alan's hand. Shocked and deterred, hardly able to use his hand, Alan resignedly returned to Base Camp.

I was spending a fair amount of time in Paul's company during these days. Without any decisions, it turned out that we were involved with similar tasks and found ourselves toiling up together several times with that rueful comradeship of the 'badly done by'. We were not badly done by, but we self-indulgently allowed ourselves to imagine that we were being Sherpas for the others. There was a solidity about Paul, a reassuring air of common sense sometimes betrayed by a manic laugh which reaffirmed his stated views on the oddity of life. Most of the times I had met Paul before the expedition had been in a pub or at parties where he would be discoursing at length, with slurred speech, on complex subjects which I failed to understand at the time and did not remember afterwards. Overall it left me with the impression that he was particularly intelligent but I could not follow what he talked about.

There was no real pairing off of anyone, but the film team, media oriented, was looking for patterns, and seeing Paul and I together on more than one day seized the opportunity to take some film of us climbing the lower slopes. Having gained some confidence about moving about on the easier ground, and familiarity with the route in the lower part of the rock buttress before the ropes started, the film crew were in the habit of venturing up themselves to find vantage points for their cameras. The debate on their role had not been concluded. There was still some uneasiness amongst the climbers about leaving the film crew alone on the mountain, and it was as difficult for us to judge how hard it was for them to cope with ground we covered as a matter of routine as it is for someone who can drive to imagine the difficulties someone sees who cannot drive. Much later, Allen Jewhurst described an incident fully justifying our fears:

> A lot of thoughts go through one's mind in fifteen seconds. Our cameraman, Mike Shrimpton, was sliding down a slope with a drop of 1,500 feet below him. We had decided to reconnoitre the route up to the Lho La and find good camera positions. It was also a reasonably safe area to see how well Graham, our sound recordist, could cope with the climbing. I had climbed the route with Peter three days earlier. After three hours we found ourselves in a disconcerting situation. At 19,000 feet we had drifted off the route and were lost. We told Graham to stay put on a rib of rock on the left of a gully. Mike was to search out to the right and I to the left. After a few minutes I recognised the route to my left, over a rise.

As I turned to call Mike, I saw him sliding down the gully. A loose rock had given way and he was falling towards Graham. Mike was a goner, I was sure, and what of Graham? If left alive with Mike dead, how would he react? Graham had never climbed in his life before and here he was at 19,000 feet with his friend falling to his death.

Graham watched astounded. Mike stretched out his arms, clawing as he fell, his fingers caught on a lip of rock and he came to a halt against Graham. With precise calmness, Mike politely told Graham to move a foot to the right. He took over Graham's perch and fifteen minutes later we were back on route with two decisions made: not to get lost again and not to tell the climbers.

Base Camp was a world away from life on the mountain; the difference was as great as that between life in Britain and life at Base Camp. For the first 1,500 feet on the ice slopes the climbers were out of sight. I had inherited the duty of making the radio calls and my conception of those on the mountain was influenced by the tiny, crackling voices which came over the radio. Without realising it, I associated the little voices with the minute figures last glimpsed through a telephoto lens, climbing slowly up to the Lho La, and half imagined my friends on the mountain to have become matchstick men. It was a foolish flight of fancy brought on by the enormity of our objective.

The twins and John arrived down with details of their progress above the Lho La and information on the line which Brian and Pete were intending to try through the rock barrier. They were awed by the effort required for the distance they had covered, by the relentless cold, even though the sky might be clear, and by the work which remained.

The film crew had an enormous lens mounted on one of their cameras and someone was forever peering through it to see if there was any sign of Brian and Pete. An excited shout went up when they were spotted; invisible to the naked eye they appeared as real people through the powerful lens, though it was only possible to distinguish them from each other by the colour of their clothing. I felt as if I was peeping in on a private, personal conflict. The two matchstick figures were close together. The red one, Brian, was above the other; from his questing movements I could see he was having difficulty. A telescoped view can be deceptive, making some things look easier, some harder; by all indications this was a crucial section with which they were struggling, and Brian described how it was.

I felt cold and quite remote from mankind. Base Camp, the tiny coloured dots on the glacier far below, was a different world. Standing here, hour after hour it seemed, as Pete led across steep ice and into the rock band, I had time to reflect on our isolation and remoteness. Already the 'norm' had become Base Camp life, a 'norm' far removed from a life surrounded by the conveniences and comforts of our civilisation.

Pete was having problems, finding himself being forced leftwards as one icy groove after another resisted his attempts to climb it. I was impatient with Pete's slow progress, feeling the urge to have a go myself and having to refrain from making what I thought would be helpful suggestions. As time passed, I became bored with the depressing scene of cloud dropping lower and lower over Pumori and Gyachung Kang, and the view down the Rongbuk glacier to the barren hills of Tibet. A twenty-six-mile marathon could be run in less time, I reflected, than it had taken us to climb up the 1,500 feet to this point.

Paradoxically, this was just the opportunity I had been waiting for. I had been ill for the first few weeks of the trip with a bronchial complaint aggravated by the dry, cold air. Plagued by an incessant cough, my role until today had been one of supporting and load-carrying for the fitter members. Illness and constant load-carrying were not what my expedition dreams were made from. Visions of surmounting difficult ice gullies, smooth slabs of rock and steep snow slopes, dreams of leading the way for rope length after rope length, had all been shattered; shattered by sickness and drudgery. Some of the team were fulfilling their dreams. I had not been, and I was questioning my own ability to cope with such a difficult route and such harsh conditions.

This time on the mountain I had started well, reaching Camp 1 quicker than I had ever done, and was enthusiastic at the prospect of breaking through the rock band. Now it was getting late, an earlier headache and grogginess had passed off but the wind was gaining in strength and the cloud was thickening. Impatience at the late hour conflicted with impatience to be leading myself. I was excited to realise that when it was my turn I should break through this impasse to the easier ground above.

With Pete finally established on a poor ledge but firmly fastened to pitons driven into rock, I followed eagerly. Where Pete had had to climb carefully, axes planted in ice, crampon points grating on rock, I, safeguarded by the rope, tried to hurry and generate some warmth. My lungs almost burst; I became light-headed and dizzy through trying to force myself without sufficient oxygen. I arrived at the ledge in a tangle of ropes. My mind was as active as a garden snail, my hands without feeling from the cold – it took a long time to untangle the ropes.

When I started up the ice gully from the ledge, the dizziness returned; I climbed more slowly. From the top of the gully, I saw the solution to the problem of surmounting the final overhangs. An undercut ledge ran left to a bottomless corner of rock. This ran up to the barrier of rock which overhung this area at the narrowest point. If I could get through the overhang here, we would be on easier ground and a major obstacle would have been conquered.

Leaving the groove I was in to gain the ledge felt extremely precarious, and the 'high' of leading was soon shattered by terror as my arms rapidly tired and the prospect of hurtling backwards down the groove loomed large. I gained the ledge with my last strength, but the strain of the previous few minutes had unnerved me so much that what I had thought a large platform now seemed barely wide enough to catch the points of my crampons. I could not rest, but clung on for dear life. 'Watch the rope, Pete,' I shouted down. 'I'll try to get a peg in.' The peg went all too easily into a crack in the rock, seeming to prise the rock away with it, but it gave me confidence and I edged left to the corner.

The corner was clogged with snow but I could rest; my terror was forgotten and I was beginning to enjoy the day. Down below it was Pete now who looked bored, fidgeting and stamping his feet impatiently. For him, I knew, time would be passing slowly. For me, time did not exist; the climbing engrossed me completely.

I cleared the snow from the corner, discovering plenty of holds, and reached the overhang quickly. After a rest, a heave upwards and a swing left landed me on the easy ground above.

There was a sense of fulfilment, a sense of achievement, but now that I was over the difficulty time did matter; night was near, wind-blown snow obscured the view down to the Lho La and the urgency of the situation made itself felt. I waited till Pete had arrived and dumped his load and we hurried off down.

Abseil followed abseil till we reached the easier slopes as darkness fell. The way back to the cave of Camp 1 was vague in the mist and dark. Several times we were blown off course by the wind and it was with relief that we chanced upon the debris of our food packages and the gentle rise up to the cave.

It was 22 December. Alan, Paul and I planned to go up the next day to take over from Brian and Pete, whom we expected to be tired after breaking through the rock barrier. I awoke on 23 December to steady snowfall and low cloud. The radio call to Pete and Brian told us that conditions were too bad to climb at the time; if the weather cleared they would do some more, if not they would enlarge the cave further and dig a snow-hole toilet, to make living conditions more bearable at Camp 1, before coming down to Base Camp. We decided not to go up ourselves until the weather cleared and I felt a guilty thrill that we might after all be at Base Camp to celebrate Christmas, and receive the next batch of mail that was due. If the weather did clear there was no question but that we would go up, whatever the sentimental attraction of celebrating Christmas, as fine days were too precious and irretrievable to pass up.

The snowfall did not let up all day; heavy, persistent flakes brought a hushed whiteness to the camp. Brian and Pete shoved their way through the drapes of the dining tent entrance towards evening, covered in snow, and still wearing crampons. Brian was gasping hard as if he had just survived an Arctic epic; Pete, controlled, strode across the tent and with measured slowness unfastened his crampons and sat down.

This was the first real encounter that any of us had had with the mountain in severe conditions and Brian's description of their descent from the snow cave gave a disconcerting impression of the forces with which we were contending.

The storm of the previous evening had worsened during the night. We guessed that no one would come up from Base Camp in such weather and Pete and I resolved to descend as quickly as possible. We did not know what it would be like to be caught in a winter storm on the mountain, and the possibility of being stranded for days seemed very real.

I left first and had difficulty standing upright against the wind as soon as I was out of the cave. The rope ran up the slope from the mouth of the cave for 200 feet to a snow stake. From there it went horizontally for another 300 feet to the first rocks from where the descent proper began. I clipped on to the rope with a clamp, which I could slide along, but which would lock on to the rope when I wanted it to. This section of slope seemed to be catching the wind at its strongest. Facing into the wind, I could not breathe, and I tried to make progress backwards. I could not keep my footing as the wind just blew me over. I went down on my knees, my head held low, and crawled up the slope. Constantly I was lifted from the ground, only to be stopped from being blown away by the rope, taut in the wind, singing under the tension.

The best method of movement was to rush and then rest. Fast movement is not easy at altitude, but movement was essential. I rested in a ball, face buried in arms, then rushed upwards for ten feet before collapsing, panting, in a crouch once more.

It was even more difficult where the ropes ran horizontally across the slope. Here I had to revert to moving backwards. The slope had steepened sufficiently to prevent me crouching in a ball and I could not face into the wind, nor could I move backwards at a rush. The force of the wind had reached a new peak and I seemed to be spending more time in mid air, like a kite, than on the surface of the snow. Even facing away from the wind it was difficult to breathe.

A vacuum was formed on the side of my body in the lee of the wind, and I was panting furiously to overcome this unexpected suffocation. With my mouth thus gaping, ice started to form inside; the cold air I was sucking into my lungs was making them ache; my whole body was cold.

Panic started to take hold of me and I tried to reason that it was not too late to turn back. I felt dizzy and lethargic as the wind pushed me, first one way, then the other and I became completely disorientated. I knew my body heat was being whipped away every second. It seemed a silly place to die, just a few rope lengths away from the safety of the cave.

My fear increased and I heard my own voice saying: 'Come on, move!' The words came out as drunken slur. I recognised that. I had reached the point where the ropes crossed a six-foot-wide crevasse mostly concealed by snow – normally a place to avoid, but now it appeared as a friend. Still attached to the rope, I launched myself into its depths and an eerie calm set in. I was still panting and disorientated but the panic had been taken out of the moment. I had time to recover and consider whether to return to the ice cave or battle on to the rocks.

Half an hour later I poked my head out into the wind, which hit me like a wall of liquid. I went for the rocks, fighting every step with my body angled at 45° into the wind. I do not remember the final hundred feet along the rope, only the sense of relief as I collapsed in the lee of the rocks.

Pete arrived after a similar struggle and my spontaneous outbursts of terror and amazement were lost in the wind; but he did not need any descriptions from me.

Lower down, we came into snowfall, the once familiar route now disguised beneath a thickening

blanket. Once easy ground was a nightmare of un-
certainty; the ropes, sometimes buried deep in the
snow, were swollen to three times their thickness
with coatings of ice. We slipped and slid downwards
for six hours, finally stumbling into Base Camp just
in time for Christmas.

Brian had some criticisms about the route up to the West Shoulder.
He felt that there had been a tendency by the twins and John to
take the most obvious line, leaving Pete and himself to sort out the
difficulties when the going became too hard. 'Let's think about it
more carefully in future,' he said.

Opinions did differ, but the main obstacle was now overcome
and it seemed good that this should have been achieved in time for
Christmas and that we should all be down together to celebrate.

7 CHRISTMAS

The abnormal darkness for the time of the morning and, above my eyes, the sagging slopes of the tent from which there came the intermittent rustle of sliding snow, told me that the camp was still enveloped in the storm we had woken to the previous day. There would be no movement upwards today either, and aware now that we would all be seeing Christmas in together I was secretly relieved. It was not good to lose a single precious day of work on the mountain but now there was no option I could relax. The significance of Christmas now permeated my consciousness and I noted in my diary: 'An unreal situation – and at the same time so normal. All the residue of Christmases past, conviviality, warmth, presents, lights, friends, girlfriends, family – and here we are, here I am, waking to snowfall and grey, heavy weather at Base Camp. The bright spot being that we are all here and the mail runner should be back today, though weather was so bad yesterday that no plane would have come in, so it will be just mail from last week.'

All day was spent in lazy preparation for a Christmas feast. We had decided to have our party, American style, on the evening of Christmas Eve, since we were all together but, if the weather improved, three of us would be leaving to go up. Suddenly I realised how much it meant to me to celebrate Christmas and how eager I was for the mail runner to arrive.

John had miraculously preserved a small supply of drink – brandy, sherry and whisky – for this occasion and some decorations and ornamental lights appeared. The dining tent took on a festive atmosphere as John, alternating between cook tent and dining tent, his face glowing more and more brightly, supervised events in the kitchen and helped himself to the chef's traditional tots of alcohol.

Five of the Japanese came over to join our celebrations. Uemura, stormbound at Camp 2, sent us Christmas greetings, and our Sherpa staff caught the spirit of our enthusiasm. Wan Chup, for once, worked willingly under John's painstaking directions.

As darkness fell on a camp blanketed in snow, trays of delicacies were ferried across into the dining tent; dressed crab, smoked oysters, paté and more sherry. The constant roar of the wind from the Lho La was drowned by the cacophany of sound from our largest cassette deck which was thrust into the bottom of an empty, drum-like container to enhance the volume.

After a while the Japanese beamed their thanks, made their excuses with inscrutable politeness and left.

The main meal, chicken, stuffing, reconstituted powdered potato and dried vegetables, arrived and more whisky was found. John had kept his *pièce de résistance* a close secret and he produced it with a flourish, flaming Christmas pud and brandy sauce. I felt bloated and content. The one flaw in the day had been the failure of the mail runner to arrive, perhaps on account of the snow.

By eight o'clock we were all laid out, drowsy and warm with the repletion of good food and drink. Stories were swapped and more banter passed around. Most of us were wearing our thick, red, down suits, making the tent seem like a gathering-place for Father Christmases. Ade, his nose a red glow, grinned mischievously and went off into a fantasy about job prospects: 'That must be a good number – being Father Christmas with all those girls that come to sit on your knee.' He and his brother now looked more alike than ever since Ade had grown a rough beard and we relished the prospect of seeing again Al's girlfriend from Kathmandu, who had written to say she would meet us on the way back.

Only Paul and Alan remained talking. Sometimes one got the impression that Alan missed the complex, intellectual discussions of his Cambridge days. Often he led the way in ribald humour, but underlying this was the suspicion of a keen intelligence which was yearning to be tested. Now Paul and Alan were locked in a discussion which centred round something about logarithmic equations inside a cube tending towards a point. Paul gave every appearance of holding his own, but to me it was totally incomprehensible and I gathered from the quizzical frown on Allen Jewhurst's face as he went off to bed that he was baffled too. I left as well and sank into a drunken sleep. Vague thoughts about the route, prompted by a starry sky, were lost in an alcoholic haze.

Perversely, the next day, Christmas Day, started fine and Paul, Alan and I made ready to go up to the Lho La. Just another work day for us and I envied those who remained their extra day of rest and celebration. It was 11 a.m. before we were ready to leave and the weather had changed. Clouds were blowing up from the south and streamers of snow were trailing off the ridge of Nuptse. There was every excuse to change plans and stay at Base but I was uncertain whether I was being influenced by common sense or the effects of the alcohol still lingering in my body. I left before delaying further and weakening. Paul and Alan, feeling no better, followed.

The well-known way up to the start of the ropes was transformed. Deep snow concealed all the familiar ledges and footholds, my hands became numb and gloves wet from the constant groping in the snow for holds. I dislodged a huge rock which lay buried and hidden, and blamed my impatience for getting ahead of the other two. I waited a long while but grew cold in the strengthening winds. I hurried on to warm up and started up the ropes of the overhanging groove without seeing Paul and Alan. From the halfway ledge I heard shouts and dimly through the swirling cloud made out a figure far below. It was difficult to hear against the noise of the wind, but it was Paul and I understood from him that he was turning back to Base Camp.

I reconsidered what I was doing. In less than an hour I would be at the snow cave; it would take longer to get back to Base Camp. I continued. The alcohol was probably still poisoning my system because the roar of the wind across the plateau above my head was like that heard inside a railway tunnel. Snow was falling thickly and it was no longer the fine day I had started, out on. We had all been lulled into a false estimation of the winter here by the relatively fine days we had experienced. I was inadequately clad, and urgently forced myself upwards before the cold penetrated to my bones. At the end of the rocks and start of the snow up and across to the cave I strapped on crampons, buffeted all the while by the wind. I could not keep my footing and pulled myself along on the slopes I had first crossed ten days ago, doubting then the necessity for fixing ropes. I reached the caves and escaped into the calmer recesses of the first one, feeling bruised, battered and exhausted. There was no sign of Alan behind me.

Pete and Brian had blocked the entrance with rucksacks but spindrift had forced its way in through every little crevice. Everything inside the cave, sleeping bags, clothes, food, was covered in a fine layer of snow. Someone's down suit was lying there so I slipped into it; mine was still over at the tent site and I did not want to venture back there. It took half an hour to clean the cave of snow, and after gathering a rucksack full of snow from outside I settled into a sleeping bag with a book.

At 6 p.m. I learnt from Ade on the radio that Alan had turned back too. Paul and Alan had both found they were going so slowly after the previous day's excesses that they were very cold and feared they should not reach the cave before dark. They had taken the safest course and retreated. I also learned that the mail runner had arrived. This completed my sense of isolation and loneliness.

'Is there any for me?' I asked hesitantly.

'Yes, I won't be able to bring any gear up tomorrow, my sack will be full of all your bloody letters. I haven't got any, I'm gonna open some of yours.'

After a few ribald comments Ade signed off. I crawled back into the cave, to spend Christmas evening on my own. I could sense a nostalgia in one part of me. I blocked it off, not thinking about who I might have letters from, forcing my thoughts into reading a rather predictable terrorist novel and made a meal, which was unenjoyable without someone to share it, last as long as possible.

The night on my own was a strange one. I blocked the cave entrance with rucksacks against the windblown snow that was billowing in. I had a suspicion that if I relaxed from a detached, unfeeling frame of mind, the bizarre nature of my situation – being alone at 20,000 feet on Everest, a mountain haunted by the ghosts of climbers dead on its slopes – might become disturbing. The cave was in sight of the spot where Mallory and Irvine had disappeared in 1924, and where their bodies may well still lie. I preferred to consider myself as being unaffected by superstition and I pushed out of my mind the sense of total loneliness which hovered on the fringes of my consciousness without the company of others to alleviate it. If I let such thoughts form and inner fears take hold, I felt they could possess and unbalance me. Sleep, once I had finished eating, came mercifully quickly and I was able to linger in an unthinking doze next morning until it was light, time to move and I could look forward to the arrival of more people and my post.

Four people arrived in the middle of the afternoon of Boxing Day – the twins, Paul and Alan – as I was finishing replacing some ropes which had become worn by the wind action rubbing them against the rock. I finished the work and joined them at the caves. I asked Ade for my mail. He looked startled and suddenly alarmed: 'I think our kid's got your letters.' He had not and I was filled with a welling resentment at their thoughtlessness. I was tempted to burst out with an attack on them for their lack of consideration but Ade looked crestfallen and was so full of self-criticism that I suppressed my annoyance. The twins are usually so thoughtful and considerate of others and they would censure themselves more heavily than I ever could, as they knew how highly prized letters are on a mountain. The fault really lay with us all, as we had no system by which messages and letters were automatically passed upwards, rather than left to the initiative of individuals.

In the morning the wind streamed strong and steady across the plateau between the caves and the slopes up to the Western Shoulder. Paul and I were to go up and complete the route through the rock barrier. Al and Ade would carry loads in support, and Alan, feeling fully recovered now, was going to make some necessary alterations to the caves.

It took half an hour, staggering in the wind, to cross the Lho La plateau. As I reached the opposite side the slope swept increasingly steeply upwards to end at a gap in the ice, the bergschrund, ten feet wide, where the angle changed abruptly and a vertical wall of ice reared up on the other side. The crevasse was unfathomably deep and it was twenty feet up the vertical wall to where the angle eased off, but a rope was in place now, stretching across the gap, up the wall, and on up the slopes above. I clipped my ascendeur device on to the rope, slid it along and swung alarmingly across the bergschrund and up the wall to the slopes above.

The wind was coming from my right, the south. The hood of my down suit projected forward round my face like blinkers on a horse. Vision was severely restricted and the wind bounced off the snow and on to my face, icicles forming from my condensed breath on beard and moustache. A long repetition of movements upward was punctuated with frequent halts to regain my breath. I was panting hard, and I found I was having to face continually to the left to avoid the discomfort of icy blasts of wind against cheeks and nose.

I was impressed with the distance up to the rock barrier; the time taken, the gruelling slog up 1,500 feet of ropes, two and a half hours from the caves to a cluster of pitons, karabiners, and spare rope left by Brian and Pete at their high point. The difficulty of climbing the rock barrier was disguised for me now the ropes were in place, but I could see why it had taken a whole day for them to climb 300 feet and marvelled at the achievement. A slight anxiety and excitement gripped my stomach in anticipation of what we would have to face.

The ropes ended at a ledge on which I crouched against the wind, peering down at the others on the slope below. Time passed; I was sitting right in the path of the wind. I hunched myself up to present as small a target as possible; the cold ate into my bones.

It seemed like hours before Paul arrived; I was numb and useless. Paul too was chilled; his feet wooden and without feeling. Should we go on or not? I did not know if I would be steady enough to lead out on new ground. The wind had been too strong to move on without someone to safeguard me with a rope. Paul vacillated, but he too wondered about the wisdom of continuing in the state we were in.

I gave it a try. Movement restored some warmth and I was able to climb upwards on a runnel of ice partially sheltered from the wind. The exposed ledge I had left was probably the worst possible place to hang around. When I had the rope anchored to an 'ice screw', driven into the solid bank of ice up which I had climbed, Paul joined me. He had not been able to regain any warmth and Ade, close behind, volunteered to take his place.

The rock barrier far exceeded in difficulty anything we could see ahead. It was not easy ground by any means but there seemed no reason for us to reach an impasse here as we had done before.

I climbed up a band of brittle ice, my crampon points fracturing and splintering the surface before finding purchase. A wind-formed ramp of snow led more easily to a slab of shattered rock into a crack in which I drove a piton. A little higher and I had reached the end of the rope. I led another 150 feet, legs straddling a shallow depression in the rock and crampons, awkward and insecure, scratching and sparking on the granite. Ade came up, tying off the rope at each anchor point I had placed and casting an appraising eye over my work. He was the only one amongst us with a guide's certificate and the lingering effects of his training still permeated his thinking.

I pressed him to lead for a while. It is much more exciting and satisfying to be out in front rather than humping a heavy load in support, though both are of equal importance. Ade unselfishly was not insisting on having a turn in front as he had done a good deal of the leading lower down. He did take over, though, and traversed diagonally rightwards up a sloping ledge of broken rocks, on and up over some black, insubstantial rock coated in ice. He made careful, measured progress for another 300 feet before the time was all eaten up and we had to descend.

Before we did, I clambered up a rib of rock for another forty feet to a vantage point from which to spy out the upper slopes. Ade followed and we were pleased to see that for the next 2,000 feet there were few obstacles comparable to the rock barrier.

We had overstayed our time limits. The sun sank behind the distant hills as we abseiled back down, casting rosy tints on the glistening ice through the rock barrier. It was dark before we wearily entered the snow caves.

Brian, Pete and John had come up earlier ferrying loads. I was surprised to find that John had not stayed, for we needed him to pair off with Al the next day so that the rest of us could have an easier day, taking our time, carrying loads in support. It seemed that there had been some dispute about movements. John had intended to stay up but Brian had insisted that there were enough people on the Lho La already, and John should stay below. There were five people at the Lho La but the work above was very demanding. The cold drained the energy and fatigue came on much more quickly than I had experienced before. The wind had a wearying effect, so it was better to keep a rotation going to replace people and distribute the work as much as possible. To have enough usable time in the day to break new ground and fix ropes we had to be up early and move fast up the already established route. Everyone else was too tired or due to descend, and I reluctantly faced the prospect of another's day exhausting work as now I would have to partner Al.

As Ade explained, this probably arose out of a discussion at Base Camp on Christmas Day. The subject had been raised about work distribution. In the absence of dictation from above, this was the democratic process at work. The twins and John were strongly of the opinion that some people were working much harder than others, whereas Pete and Brian were just as convinced that everyone had done about the same. Alan was convinced that everyone was working to his own personal limit, which was all that could be expected or was possible. Since no one wanted to establish a formal rota, clashes of opinion were inevitable.

Al and I did not do so much the next day. I was tired and left the cave late. It was not such easy ground as first thought and I found Al to be super-cautious, and his comments suggested that he found my methods to be on the careless side. Climbing back up to the previous day's high point, I was hard-pressed to keep up with his purposeful, steady pace. He followed the Diemberger theory that maintains that slow, no matter how slow, but constant movement is the best way to achieve progress at altitude. I could not stand the tedium of constant movement and when Al glanced back to see how I was doing I shouted up to him that I preferred 'interval training' – actually preferring the intervals to the training,

We ran out nearly 500 feet of rope and Paul and Alan toiled up as we finished for the day with heavy loads of rope and a tent. It was dark again before we regained the cave after a wild sunset.

At last my mail had arrived. There was a card for Christmas from Maria showing a chorus line of eight buxom girls from the thirties, and the back of the card was smothered with the lipstick-imprinted shapes of different lips. Alan was disgusted that I could not tell which were Maria's. There was also a letter from my mother saying she was having a Mass said at Christmas for our safe return. This made a remarkable impression on everyone.

John was now here to stay, Brian and Pete were due to come up the next day, so Alan, Paul, Al and I descended. It was hard to sustain the energy to do anything effective for more than a couple of days without a rest and decent food. There was plenty of food in the caves but cooking a meal was a three-hour task and there was a tendency to miss out on eating and succumb to the constant feeling of lassitude induced by the altitude.

It was a stormy morning; the wind drove flurries of snow into the caves; John and Ade kept poking their heads out and trying to decide what to do. John wanted to go to find out what it was like to climb in really bad conditions. Ade, more cautious, did not want to waste a day battling upwards only to be driven back and be too tired to utilise the next day should it be fine.

I met Brian and Pete, coughs still troubling them, as I went down. The roar of the wind became more faint as I got lower and I felt with surprise the sun's warmth when it peeped through the clouds. The mountain was still wrapped in a swathe of cloud, still ravaged by the winds, a microcosm of turbulent weather all to itself.

In four nights I had become conditioned to accepting constant wind and cold. Base Camp was luxury by comparison. I revelled in the warmth of a sun that cast splendid light on the pinnacles and blocks of ice which reared up out of the glacier. A footpath had been trodden through the new snow that was painfully bright.

The mail runner had already left but I busied myself with writing cards and letters, an occupation made unpleasant by the cracks and sores in my fingers. The constant cold and necessity to handle rough objects lacerates the fingers and the cuts often turn septic. It was painful even to hold a pen. Graham, the sound man from the film crew, had slight frostbite in one of his fingers.

Of the three film-crew, Graham was the least certain about making this film. He was the quietest member of our whole group, often spending hours at a time without saying a word, soaking up with amazement the many tales of adventure and lawlessness which dominated conversations. After one series of stories from which one could only deduce that the streets inhabited by the Burgess twins were pregnant with violence, Graham did interject a wry comment of 'Yes, I can't walk down a street in Harrogate without thinking someone's going to jump me from a doorway.'

On another occasion Al, after reading a book about a con-man who drugged and murdered his victims, questioned Pete about whether there was an antidote if one felt a strange drowsiness creeping over one and suspected poison. Al saw such knowledge as relevant to his own life-style. Graham parodied him with a bubbling smile: 'Is there anything you can take, Pete, if you feel the point of a knife in your back? Anything to stop that taking effect?'

Graham had gone up on to the lower slopes with Allen and Mike to do some filming and sound recording. For the climbers, being filmed made little difference except that it took longer to get from one place to another as we were often asked to repeat a section so that it could be filmed from a different angle. The film crew were static for most of the time and even when the sun was out the actual air temperature was still well below zero. Only movement kept one warm. One day Graham's feet and hands were numb without him realising it. Once numb, they can freeze solid without one knowing. It is only while one feels the cold that one knows there is still blood circulating and sensation still there.

Without knowledge of all these details Graham was not aware

of anything except that he was more clumsy at handling things and it was only on returning to Base, where his hands and feet thawed out and pain came with the returning sensation as the blood tried to revive the dying tissue, that he realised his toes were 'frost-nipped', that is in the first stages of frostbite, and he spent many hours standing up, stamping his feet up and down to induce warmth and clasping his hands in his armpits. Graham found he could hardly eat any of the food, just the smell of it revolting him. This was a feature of living at altitude and is not uncommon. He seemed to shrink visibly before our eyes and having weighed himself on some scales at the Japanese camp found that he had lost two stones in weight.

During these days a visitor arrived, an Australian who had braved the rigours of winter to come up to Base Camp, relying upon us to feed and shelter him. It is part of the agreeable spirit of the mountains that such hospitality should be shown, but I did feel he took too much for granted and found that I resented the intrusion into our private world as much as if I walked into my house to find a complete stranger making himself at home and asking questions about my private affairs. I realised that I had come to terms completely with our life in the mountains and felt like an animal in a zoo when anyone came to stare and probe with questions.

He did, however, bring disturbing news. He had been at Lobuje and seen our mail runner offering for money to the Sherpani who ran the tea house, packets of biscuits and bags of coffee which could only have come from our food store. This further evidence of dishonesty amongst our staff revived anger which is more virulent for being aroused by the behaviour of someone to whom one has shown particular friendship. It seemed to emphasise the distance, which exists in those inscrutable beings behind the flashing smiles, between them and us. The mail runner's job is particularly important and dependent on honesty, and once more we had to approach Mr Singh and ask that someone be dismissed.

Our shy Liaison Officer was being asked to perform some unpleasant duties. We were still no closer to him than at the start of the expedition. He had his own routine for the day and only ate with us because we insisted on it, though after a while we realised he preferred the extremely hot and highly spiced food of the Sherpas. He only spoke when spoken to and he answered my provocative attempts at getting him to open up more with the patient air of a teacher handling a troublesome schoolboy.

'Wales is part of Great Britain like Nepal is part of India,' I said in a deliberately outrageous answer to one of his questions.

'Mr Joe, you are always teasing me,' he replied. 'Nepal is not part of India. It is independent country.'

Alan hooted with laughter at this and congratulated Mr Singh on having got my measure.

Later on a murmur of anticipation went through the camp as the mail runner was spotted. Being British and reserved, and the twins, our strong-arm men, being away on the hill, we felt some embarrassment about how to handle the situation. Mr Singh, a changed man as he took on his role of policeman, called the mail runner over to his tent.

There is usually an implicit welcome and congratulation to the mail runner on his arrival, and the contrast this time was wounding. None of us could understand the exchanges which took place, but we gathered that the mail runner had brought back some of the biscuits and coffee he had been seen trying to sell, saying that he had taken them in mistake for some other food the cook had instructed him to have for his journey. The Liaison Officer did not accept this, for he believed that the mail runner had been warned by some yak herders who had brought wood and food up to the Japanese camp and called in to ours before going down.

An argument erupted, the Liaison Officer leapt to his feet and lashed out at the mail runner who took off down the glacier. The rest of us, film team included, stood there open-mouthed and helpless at this scene. After a long while the Liaison Officer, extremely agile in pursuit, brought down the mail runner and proceeded to rain blows on him. A very subdued Sherpa was led back to camp and sat abjectly in front of the tent where Mr Singh sat in judgement. Tears flowed down the cheeks of the mail runner as the sentence of dismissal was pronounced and the retraction of all the much valued clothing and equipment was made. It was another unpleasant incident which took the pleasure out of the arrival of the mail.

Base Camp no longer seemed a place to relax. The visitor who had reported the mail runner's dishonesty had gone but returned with a group of trekkers he had persuaded to come up to enjoy the hospitality of our expedition. It was an added burden to our cook staff. When the visitors asked questions and made suggestions about the climb I felt it an unwarranted intrusion into a very personal, intimate matter. Most of them were ill-equipped to deal with the savage conditions of Base Camp life and had to borrow clothes and tents to survive. I was unashamedly glad to see them go.

On the mountain we followed progress via the radio and tele-photo lens. The matchstick figures were on the vast snow slope leading to a ridge of rock at the top of which we hoped to find a sheltered campsite.

On New Year's Day Alan, Paul and I set off back to the Lho La. We did some filming on the way up but I did not feel too good. Whether it was ennui at finding myself going over the same ground for the ninth time, slight sickness or the subconscious wish not to miss out on another celebration day I could not ascertain. After talking with Paul I dumped my load and hurried down to catch up with Mike and Allen who were making their way back to camp. They were surprised to see me and shamefacedly I explained to them that it just was not going well for me that day, so we returned together. I felt as if I had given myself a holiday. On passing through the Japanese camp we were summoned inside for some of their celebratory New Year drink and tasty morsels of yak meat cooked in tiny slivers over their wood stove.

The Base Camp was empty except for the film crew and myself. The cook and one cook boy had gone down to Namche Bazaar to organise the transportation of some essentials of which we had run short. Only one of the Sherpa boys remained and he produced an excellent evening meal. There was a peace and tranquillity that had been missing for the last few days, and the four of us made a small enough group for warm, meaningful chatter until late into the night.

Graham informed us that the Japanese had reported finding Yeti footprints in the Western Cwm, where they had their Camps 1 and 2. They had filmed them and sent the film back to Japan. We were highly sceptical. I felt much better on 2 January and went up on my own, gathering extra items on the way and labouring up with a particularly heavy sack as a self-imposed punishment for the weakness of the previous day.

8   GRIM NIGHTS

The site for Camp 2 had been reached. Twenty-eight rope lengths, over 4,000 feet of rope fixed in place, stretched up from the plateau of the Lho La to a twisting rib of rock a thousand feet below the crest of the West Shoulder. That distance was quite far enough between camps, any further would have produced a diminishing return in that so much effort was being expended in just reaching the top of the ropes that if the camp was located any higher, a day's rest might have become necessary to regain strength after reaching Camp 2.

Pete and Ade had run out the final rope lengths, but there had been some conflict over the roles of those active on the hill, as I learnt on reaching Camp 1. Ade and John had climbed together one day and intended to do so on the next day. Brian and Pete were carrying loads in support. Pete was annoyed at the assumption that he would play a supporting role on two days running, and he protested strongly that he was not only a doctor but also a climber and that there was no point in his being on the mountain if he was not to have his share of the more interesting business of leading.

John and Ade worked on the assumption that it was better for those who were fittest to do the work which demanded most effort and since Pete had been a long way behind them whilst they were leading it seemed most efficient to continue in the lead themselves.

John has a preference for avoiding confrontation, for withdrawing from an argument to preserve the peace even though he is not convinced of the other view. When Pete maintained that he was climbing as well and as fast as anyone, John stood down and let Pete partner Ade next day.

This disagreement typified the difficulties of a democratically organised expedition; we all had differing views and opinions. Ade did not like to see decisions being made out of, as he saw, a sense of personal pique and he bluntly told Pete that he did not expect to be kept waiting. If Pete was as fit as anyone, he should reach the high point at the same time as Ade himself.

Pete Thexton was the least known to anyone on the trip. He had an individualist streak in him, preferring to walk on his own and to go off for solitary excursions. So far I had not been impressed with his performance; in comparison to the twins, in spite of the charts he kept of everyone's movements, he had done considerably less. It came as a disturbing surprise to hear of his forceful demands when the twins were characterised by a selfless application to whatever task arose.

On the day they set off together, Ade arrived at the top of the ropes long before Pete and, since it was relatively easy ground, laid in place another 300 feet of rope before Pete arrived. They completed together another 600 feet of climbing before finding a place suitable for a camp.

John and Ade descended to Base Camp as I came up. Al and Paul had gone up to pitch a tent at Camp 2 and Ade suggested that Alan and I did the same. After a comfortable night at Camp 1, in the now familiar caves, Alan and I set off for Camp 2. Brian and Pete were going to carry a load up and then descend to Base Camp for a rest while we continued with the route.

I like to be either at the back of a group or well ahead. When every step is an effort it is difficult to match one's pace to another person's and if I am in front I tend to assume that those behind could move faster but for my holding them up. If at the back I can make my own pace. On this occasion I got well ahead, counting off each rope as I left it. Twenty-eight rope lengths seemed endless, but the first fourteen were the worst – 4,000 feet of slow, upward trudging, facing away from the wind. I expected to arrive in mid-afternoon at Camp 2. The weather was not fine.

Clouds covered the sky, streaming rapidly from the crest of the West Shoulder. The wind sometimes threw me off balance and I looked forward to settling into a tent when I reached the campsite.

Paul and Al were surprised when I arrived, being convinced that the weather was too foul for anyone to think of coming up. Consequently there was no platform dug ready for a second tent. I took it for thoughtlessness and told them so. They had had a bad night in the coffin-like confines of the box tent. Paul and Al were both big and broad-shouldered; in the tent they were too squashed against each other to rest properly. There was only one door which opened directly on to the outside and to cook they had the choice of keeping the door zipped closed and suffocating from the fumes from the stove or leaving it open and being covered in snow from the icy blasts of the wind.

Even if the weather had been better, both Al and Paul were suffering too much from lack of sleep and the constant buffeting they had felt from the wind through the tent walls. The only virtue of the tent was that it had very thick poles and seemed proof against the wind.

I set to with some annoyance to dig a platform out of the slope directly above the box tent. Paul cursed me and explained, with common-sense arguments, that I was knocking down great chunks of snow and ice which were building up behind his tent and forcing it off its platform. I was frantic at the thought of being caught by nightfall without a well-erected tent, long icicles hung from my moustache and beard and my hands were numb. Clouds concealed even the cheering brightness of the sun and snow stung my face.

Paul came up to help me erect the tent, one I had used in ferocious weather on K2 and had every confidence in. Now I could not manage it at all. The savage wind kept grabbing at the tent; I tried and failed many times to locate the poles in the necessary places. Paul held on but I was the only one who had used these tents, had sung their praises and now could not expect more than minimal help as the method of erecting it was too complicated to be passed on when every shouted word was snatched away by the wind. I bent one of the aluminium tubes into place to form an arc from which the tent would hang. The pole snapped. I felt a fool for advocating the use of this tent. The weather on K2 had been terrible, but the quality of the cold on Everest was much more severe. My useless hands fumbled with other poles as I tried various ways of botching up my blunder. Paul watched with mute, helpless interest. With the poles finally in place I suspended the light inner tent from the arcs formed and turned to pulling the orange outer tent over the framework. It is the outer tent which gives the structure strength. When properly in place the arcs hold the outer skin in tension and a stable dome is formed. The last manoeuvre of pulling the outer tent over the end of the pole is hardest and in my struggles, with the tent lifting in the air, another pole snapped. I was furious but allowed my fury to rage without stopping my movements for a moment. Brian appeared, dropped his load, and grabbed the tent too.

It was not a perfect job, but when we had finished the tent was upright and, for the moment, withstanding the wind. We drove stakes into the snow to anchor the tent and buried the edges with blocks of ice and more snow. I dived inside, Paul scuttled off to his own tent and Brian hurried back down to Camp 1. These slopes were no place to linger needlessly, and tears were already forming in my eyes at the pain of frozen fingers returning to life.

Alan arrived late in the afternoon and settled into the tent with me. The icy platform beneath the ground sheet was uneven, and near the edge it was insubstantial. The useable floor space of an already tiny tent was much reduced. We both shuffled into sleeping bags and, pressed close against each other, tried to impose some sort of order on to the chaos of food and gear strewn inside the tent. If it was not done before dark we would have no hope of locating anything we needed.

An icy layer began to form on the inside surface of the tent fabric as the condensation from our breathing came into contact with the cold material and froze. It was 5 p.m. and almost dark before we were reclining in uncomfortable readiness to prepare the evening meal. Suddenly we heard the slow, rhythmic crunch of footsteps outside and the sound of Pete coughing; he had just arrived.

'Pete, it will be dark soon, what are you doing up here?'

He had set off with a load, as we knew, but, instead of descending in time to regain Camp 1 before dark, had continued. There was no sleeping bag for him and no room. He had on his down suit, the normal clothing up here, but it was so cold that a sleeping bag as well was necessary to survive the night.

'Oh, I'll be all right.'

He seemed unconcerned and passed by to visit Al and Paul at the other tent. I was amazed when he did not leave for another half hour. There were ropes all the way down to the level plateau of the Lho La but in the dark it is so easy to make a fatal mistake.

'Have you got a torch?'

'Yeah, I'll be all right,' he repeated and crunched off. Alan looked at me with incomprehension and shook his head.

The tent we were in differed from the box tent occupied by Al and Paul in that there was an inner tent and outer shell. The outer shell came right down to floor level and had a flap on which we had placed blocks of ice and snow. We could thus open the doors on the inner tent without the wind blowing in. This enabled us to collect snow to melt and allowed us to ventilate the tent whilst cooking.

Hoar-frost formed a thickening layer on every surface; a dangling piece of nylon cord grew to three times its usual size with the accumulation of ice crystals on it. Outside the wind swept ceaselessly across the ice slope into which we had cut a slot for the tent.

Each gust which shook the tent sent down showers of ice, and undermined any confidence in it surviving the night. One of us had to be attentive to the stove the whole time to prevent it overturning and soaking clothes and food. It was a wretched, squalid scene.

I was too uncomfortable to sleep easily and the noise from the wind banging at the tent kept me in a state of nervous anticipation. The box tent was twenty feet below but communication was impossible. Alan has the enviable ability of relaxing and sleeping in the most painful circumstances, an accomplishment which he attributes to his drunken youth at Cambridge when he frequently spent the night where he fell. I needed a sleeping pill to block out the discomfort and anxiety.

The whole of the next day was spent enlarging the tent platform and building a protective wall of snow blocks as a wind break. There was no let up in the ferocious buffeting of the wind and stinging snow flurries; no opportunity for consultation; each person did what he thought best. Al felt ill after two successive nights of disturbed sleep and insufficient food. He shuffled off down.

Our purpose in being at Camp 2 was to continue upwards but until we had a comfortable camp we could do little and against this wind there was no hope of progress. All efforts were focused on merely surviving the savage, inescapable cold. The tents seemed like flies against the massive wind which battered the mountain. I was incapable of undressing sufficiently to relieve myself, the cold was so severe.

In the midst of another wretched night I awoke in terror feeling snow on my face and in the bewilderment between nightmare and wakefulness shook Alan and asked if he was all right. It was the recurring nightmare which had troubled me ever since the avalanche high on K2. The sensation I had experienced on waking to find snow pouring remorselessly down and crushing me under a black, soundless blanket before losing consciousness, had left a lasting mark on my psyche.

Alan reassured me that nothing had changed. The tent was still shaking in the wind and a torch, shone inside, showed the constant showers of hoar-frost which fell from a layer a quarter-inch thick which covered the walls and roof. Alan had a rough night which left him listless and weary next day. He descended to Camp 1 to escape for a while from the horror of life at Camp 2. Paul came by a little later. He too felt dreadful after a third night spent in the path of the winds. Even though the wind did not penetrate the tents, the noise wore on the nerves and there was the ever-present anxiety that the fabric of the tent would tear or the poles would break. Inside the tents the air temperature varied between -30 degrees Celsius and -40 degrees Celsius. A stove did not seem to make any difference, we had to wear gloves the whole time, and rather than raise the temperature a stove only increased the depth of hoar-frost which formed inside the tent.

I shared a drink I had ready with Paul, who described the discomfort of the box tent before descending to the secure caves of Camp 1, and I was left alone.

Alone again on this hostile mountain. I wrote in my diary, which had become little more than a series of notes to mark the passage of time: 'On most mountains there is some respite; once on the Lho La there is a constant battering of the psyche and body by the wind and cold. It really is grim waking up here to a tent coated with rime.'

A weak sun made a pale appearance through the clouds but the rime never left the tent all day. I wondered what I could do. Camp 2 was at 22,500 feet; I considered going on my own to survey the ground above or dropping back to bring up some rope and equipment which had accumulated at various points on the way. Being left alone took the urgency out of doing anything, and since each time I opened the tent door a swirling cloud of snow blew in, I let the day slip away completely without stirring outside.

There was no radio at Camp 2 and no means of guessing the movements of anyone else. The cold and altitude had a numbing effect on my sensitivity as well as my flesh. I did not stir from my sleeping bag all day, welcoming the extra space now that Alan had gone, and drifted periodically in and out of sleep, like someone in a hospital bed. No one else arrived that day and as dark came on I prepared a solitary meal which I ate as a duty.

I took two sleeping pills to wipe out my stark surroundings but was woken at 10 p.m. by the crash of wind against the tent. I lay for the rest of the night listening and worrying whether the tent would hold. Morning was welcome for the arrival of light but the wind did not lessen; I was too fatigued to make any progress outside, and reluctant to undergo the chore of stowing all the gear strewn inside the tent and face the unpleasantness of descending to Camp 1.

I can no longer remember the experience of being alone; I find it hard to comprehend that I spent three days without stirring above the tent at Camp 2. Like the gum anaesthetised by the dentist's needle, insensitive but not dead, I performed the minimum necessary to survive but languished in comatose inactivity whenever possible. Three days and no possibility, no thought of upward movement. I did not miss the company of others but noticed the passage of time in which I had not said a word. Sometimes I did think aloud but cut off any philosophical musings which probed the sense of what I was doing.

By early afternoon, having glimpsed the mental lassitude which can induce the physical paralysis leading to death, I had resolved to escape downwards. I packed gear into rucksacks which I placed outside into a maelstrom of snow, found the lifeline of rope, and headed down. My legs, unaccustomed after my confinement to exercise, collapsed under me as I slid down the ropes and my hands fumbled weakly at each knot. When I reached the level plateau of the Lho La, standing freely for the first time in days, I dropped one of my ascendeurs which slid down a slight incline for fifty feet. I was too tired to go after it. Stumbling and falling, I made my way back against the wind to the snow caves.

Innumerable accidents occur when people become separated or isolated on a mountain. In the prevailing wild weather, Paul and Alan were anxious lest I should try to fight my way down alone or remain trapped for days if no one else could get up.

'It's all right leaving someone on his own if you want an exciting story to take back,' said Alan, 'but not if you want to climb a mountain safely.'

I relaxed into the security of the cave as Alan prepared endless drinks and food, which he passed over to Paul and me. We had done no more than spend a few days at 22,500 feet but we felt as if we had survived a traumatic ordeal and could luxuriate in the relative comfort of this Camp 1 cave. The temperature inside was -10 degrees Celsius.

Later in the afternoon John arrived and the sight of the three of us languishing in sleeping bags brought on a torrent of recrimination from him. He was highly critical of the lack of progress above Camp 2, and censorious of the amount of food we were consuming whilst lying inactive at Camp 1.

With the slow deliberation of the self-righteous I explained to him the conditions we had experienced, and gradually it sank into John that the sunny days he had been enjoying at Base Camp bore no relation to the brutal life on the mountain. Contrite and apologetic, John agreed that he was 'sounding off a bit' without sufficient awareness of our situation.

Ade was also meant to be coming up with Mike, the camera-man; John had last seen them doing some filming in the over-hanging groove. Mike had done some rock climbing in Britain but even though we had ropes in place all the way to the cave now we preferred that one of us should be with him on the mountain as much as possible. The amount of camera equip-ment that was accumulating at the Lho La was alarming; it clear-ly showed the differences of emphasis between the climbers and the film crew. I felt strongly that not a single day should be lost in climbing the mountain through attention to the film.

By dark the fierce winds still ripped across the slopes outside and there was no sign of Ade and Mike. The never distant unease surfaced. I left the warmth of my sleeping bag, fastened on my harness and crawled out into the night. I could not stand in the wind. I clipped some ascenders to the anchored rope and pulled myself up the incline. After 100 feet the ropes crossed the slope horizontally but still I could not stand. I crawled on all fours, my harness fastened to the rope by the ascender which allowed me to pull myself forward without sliding back. I couldn't see in the dark, I couldn't look up into the wind without my face being stung with snow and numbing instantly. It was only 300 feet to the rocks at the far side and three times I was picked up and thrown up the slope by the force of the wind. I felt idiotic and presumptuous against such power. I descended to the top rim of the amphitheatre and peered into the dark; no sight, no sound above the wind. I shouted uselessly and turned back.

At the far side of the traverse across the slope a shadowy figure, cowled and ominous, stood waiting. It was Paul, his back to the wind, waiting to make sure I was safe. No word passed, we descended to the cave and in the calm inside I told them. I had found nothing.

A radio call at 6 p.m. to Base Camp revealed that they had not arrived back. We arranged a recall at 7 p.m. and with relief heard that Ade and Mike had appeared ten minutes earlier. I always have a slight sense of foolishness as if I have been over-reacting in such situations, but to wait until one is sure that something has gone wrong is to invite tragedy.

We spent a restless night; the roof of the cave seemed to lift with the force of the wind, ear drums popped with the sudden pressure changes as the wind hammered at the entrance, the thump of the blasts kept everyone's nerves on edge.

Morning brought no change. We concocted a meal from freeze-dried scrambled egg mixed with chunks of tinned ham. It tasted almost like real food.

By 1 p.m. we were too tired and dispirited to stay up any longer. The weather showed no signs of improvement and I radioed down our decision.

Once at the top of the corner I slid down away from the constant roar which had been with me for days – it was like a climatic deconditioning process. A thousand feet lower and a parting in the clouds let sunlight filter through and warm my body and I began to relax and the tension of the last few days ebbed away. These walls of rock which had taken all our efforts were now reassuring and pleasant to pass over. I realised that I had not relieved myself for three days and a sudden overwhelming urge forced me to rip open my harness, down suit and underclothes to release three days of constipation just in time.

9 'IN THE MOUNTAINS ONE FORGETS TO COUNT THE DAYS'

There was a poor bag of mail waiting for us. Alan fretted at the continued lack of letters from his girlfriend. I tried to reassure or commiserate with him since I had not had a letter from Maria for three weeks, nor from my mother, who writes dutifully every Sunday. My attempt at reassurance had the opposite effect. Alan just thought I was more inhuman and unfeeling than him. On expeditions I had come to make a deliberate point of not letting emotional events affect me. I feel the lack of letters deeply but to worry about what might or might not be happening in another way of life is to conjure up a punishing fantasy world which can disturb one's thoughts and influence one's decisions. For many years whilst I trained to be a Catholic priest I lived in a dream world, planning for the holidays when I could really live, escaping mentally from the strait-jacket of a rigid timetable, strict rules and enforced behaviour. Having left that regime, I had an antipathy towards any tendency to live in fantasy worlds, preferring to think only about what I knew I could do and not to live in hope only to be disappointed or to find that the reality did not live up to my dreams.

On an expedition I exercised a possibly harmful capacity for viewing situations and events from my other life in a detached, anaesthetised manner. Of late, expeditions had gone on for a long time and on returning to England I found it took me quite a while before I regained the habit of feeling and emotion. This was very difficult for anyone close to me.

The heavy snows we were experiencing were affecting flights to Syangboche; from where our mail was collected. This was one reason for the small offering brought by the mail runner.

A party of eight Italians had arrived and made a Base Camp near ours. They were intending to climb Lhotse, the fourth highest mountain in the world, by the route which had defeated the Poles in 1974/75. They were a jolly bunch, a little disconcerted by the rigours of winter and concerned that their clothing was not adequate. They brought a comment from Reinhold Messner, who had climbed Everest twice without oxygen, and who is regarded as something of a god in Italy. He considered it impossible to climb the mountain in winter without oxygen.

I believed that he would have produced a different opinion if he had set his mind to attempting just that. Part of the reason for our being on Everest in winter was to find out what was possible.

It was true that some discouragement prevailed in our camp. The long spells of fine weather from December were gone, and any forecast picked up on Radio Nepal only spoke of winds of 100 knots, sometimes 120 knots, precipitation and cloud. The forecasts were of little help. In contrast to other seasons, the weather seemed to change radically in a very short space of time and without warning. The Japanese expedition was also having difficulty contending with the unpredictable arrival of sudden snow storms.

Life was comparatively easy physically at Base Camp and mentally relaxing for me with the knowledge that for the moment I was due a rest. A book I was reading, written in the style of Hemingway, about the Caribbean, sub-aqua escapades and cocktails on hotel verandas at sunset contrasted dreamily with our spartan existence. I missed a radio call one morning because I had left the set outside my sleeping bag and the batteries were cold. Normally I slept with the radio close to my body to keep it operable. My camera too had to be kept in my sleeping bag and I often dropped off to sleep in the escapist cocoon of sound on the headphones of a tiny Sony cassette deck, which was also pushed down into the warmth.

From Base Camp I could see through the powerful telephoto lens that the tents at Camp 2 were still in place, but on the radio we learnt that no one had yet moved up there. A whole day had been spent assisting Mike with his loads of film equipment up to the Lho La and more gear had still to be collected from where it had been dumped. This was just what we had been wary of, having to spend valuable time shepherding one of the film crew up or down the mountain. There was a clear conflict of interests between the demands of the film and the needs of the climb. Lost days were irreplaceable and although we could not reasonably leave any of the film crew to move about on their own on any difficult sections this had to be the last time that efforts to climb the mountain were distracted by the film. I felt an infuriating annoyance at what seemed to be such an obvious mistake in priorities.

Al and I planned to go back up the next day, 10 January. Paul and Alan were afflicted by a return of the dysentery which had lingered round our camp and needed a little more rest.

Life at Base Camp had settled into a routine. There were no more problems with the staff except that the food did not have the same variety or taste as it had had during the approach march. The cook was battling against adverse circumstances in trying to produce palatable food on the temperamental stoves. Even the custard which was produced was uncooked or burnt. We summoned Mingma, the cook boy, to complain, as custard is the easiest thing in the world to make. He did not seem well suited to have his efforts rejected. With bad grace he took back the custard, taking a flying kick at some broken stoves which lay outside.

Al kept us entertained with another story of bewildered involvement in violence from an occasion when he and his brother, on a rare visit home, had taken their mother out for a meal. On leaving the restaurant to drive home they found that someone had broken into the car and was sitting in the driver's seat ready to drive off. As he described it I could visualise the two of them moving into action as in a scene from a gangster movie.

'I was a bit worried about what to do,' said Al.

'Why? Were you frightened?'

'No, it's just that you never know what your mother is going to think, do you? We just roughed him up a little bit.'

On the return to Camp 1 for once I was moving faster than Al, but I suspected that he had a heavier load than me. To gain the slopes leading up to where we had ropes in place we had to cross beneath the threatening walls of ice hanging below the Lho La. It only took fifteen to twenty minutes to pass over the exposed area and there were two schools of thought about the best line to take. In 1978 I had seen a monumental avalanche from the Lho La. All seemed quiet in winter but I chose to take an indirect line that entailed an uncomfortable scramble for a long way up the unstable rocks skirting the glacier. The Burgess twins, exponents of fitness and speed, took a line for as far as possible up a gully directly in the fall line from the ice walls. They maintained that they could run to one side out of the way of anything falling. We came to call their way the 'Burgess couloir'. I told them that I would rather take ten minutes longer to get up the mountain than present the slightest opportunity of being caught in an avalanche. The other members of the team oscillated between the two schools of thought.

It was not unusual for me to part amicably from other people and wend a separate way up to where we picked up crash helmets and harnesses to start the more difficult climbing.

Mike Shrimpton was in residence at the caves filming our approach and clearly awed by his surroundings. Ade and John, Pete and Brian had gone on up to Camp 2 that day.

For the rest of the afternoon we lay inside the cave in sleeping bags, discussing the route, the film and climbing in general. Mike questioned us on our ideas for a title for the film. 'How about "Everest – Another Pawn in the Game"?' He was trying to locate the significance of trying to climb Everest by even harder, ever different routes, and our reasons for doing it. I did not think it was a very compelling title, nor that it did justice to the continual development of climbing exploring the frontiers of the possible.

Al and I promised to rendezvous with Mike next day in the afternoon when the light was good as we descended from carrying loads up to Camp 2. We intended to reclimb the rock barrier so that Mike could film it. Mike had begun to appreciate some of the problems we had raised when he was proposing the film equipment he would like on the mountain. He had the biggest movie camera I had ever seen outside of picture books as it was and he was still not satisfied with the tripod I had carried up with great effort.

Mike was a real professional. As the expedition had gone on I had acquired an increasing respect for his energy and thoroughness in tackling his job. The television industry is hamstrung by union regulations and conditions and sometimes I wondered how Mike came to terms with the subconscious demands this background made on him. There was no conceivable way in money terms that anyone could be compensated for putting up with the conditions on Everest in winter. We had had problems in the first place owing to union rules that stated we should take along an electrician whose job is to set up and plug in the lighting. The fact that there was no electric power source on Everest carried no weight and the thousands of extra pounds which a surplus film crew member would entail resulted in our making the film as an independent enterprise.

Mike was on Everest because he wanted to be there, and the breadth of his experience as cameraman on 'Whicker's World', Arthur C. Clarke's 'Mysterious World' and many other assignments which had taken him to most countries in the world gave him a maturity and broad-minded vision which was an asset to the team as a whole.

The next day we were planning would be a demanding and exhausting one but if successful would mean that a major part of Mike's filming programme on the mountain was completed. Thereafter smaller cameras handled by the climbers were to be used. We talked late into the night before snuggling down into sleep.

We were woken in the middle of the night by the unnerving thump of the wind driving, in powerful gusts, into the snow cave entrance; the increase in pressure made our ear drums pop, and thereafter I was awake for the rest of the night, vaguely aware of the restlessness of Al and Mike, lying listening to the frightening roar of the wind outside. The thump of the wind and subsequent pressure waves were as I imagined it to be in a bunker under mortar attack. We were quite secure, in my mind I knew, but the four others had gone up and were occupying the fragile tents of Camp 2. I could not imagine the tents surviving such winds. Anxiously we awaited the radio call at 7 a.m.

I crouched in the entrance of the cave, buffeted by a wind which seemed to have concrete solidity, holding on to an axe driven into the ice as I called up Camp 2 on the radio. No reply. Every half hour I opened up the radio, hoping for some sign that the four at Camp 2 were alive. At eight thirty the radio crackled in reply. Ade was saying something about a tent being destroyed in the wind then the message came to a strangled end. Uneasily I conveyed the news to Al and Mike and periodically we crawled along the tunnel entrance to peer at the slopes of ice, glimpsed through swirling cloud, waiting for a sight of figures descending and the relief that this would bring.

At 10 a.m. I saw a figure through a telephoto lens moving hurriedly downwards. Ade arrived, instantly reassuring us that no accident had happened, and John followed some time later. All were safe but the collapse of the tent had thrown John and Ade on the mercy of the wind. John's hands had frozen solid and, near fainting with pain from the cold, he had pushed himself into the cramped confines of the still standing box tent where Brian and Pete had a pan of tea heating. John thrust his hands into the hot liquid and gradually the circulation returned.

Ade reckoned that the box tent would stand against the wind but Brian and Pete were finding life quite miserable inside. Every gust of wind showered them with the ice which lined the tent. He did not know whether they planned to stay up at Camp 2.

Disconsolate and bewildered, we retired to our sleeping bags and lay all day listening to the howling wind outside, feeling the thud of impact when it drove into the entrance.

Brian and Pete appeared out of the swirling mist towards late afternoon and occupied the other cave with John. Morale was at a low ebb and progress against such savage, elemental fury seemed impossible.

Ade explained that the wind had somehow got underneath the tent, lifted it up and snapped the poles. Fortunately this had happened at 6 a.m., just before dawn. The chaos of such an event in the full dark of night was too frightening to contemplate.

Ade was tired; we fed him drinks and food, and he dozed on

and off. In the course of the afternoon we discussed our chances on the mountain. Ade was of the opinion that we had no hope of making any significant progress from the tents. Even if they withstood the wind it was not possible to rest well enough to do a day's work. Spending a night in the tent took all one's energy. He suggested a snow cave as the only possible solution.

Time seemed to be running out on us. Camp 2 had first been reached eleven days before and since then all eight of us had spent some time in the tents without moving any further up the mountain. I suggested siting a cave 1,000 feet higher where the slopes eased off before the final crest of the shoulder. I had come round to accepting a point of view I had been against earlier because of the effort involved. Al and I agreed to go up, put up with the discomfort of the box tent, and work regardless of the weakening effects of the altitude and discomfort until there was some semblance of a cave for the next party to occupy. We would have to descend after this as, even if all went well, we would be exhausted after such sustained work, but it presented the only chance of establishing a secure foothold high on the mountain. With a cave higher than the tent site we hoped to avoid placing another camp before 25,000 feet, thus cutting down on some of the time and effort. It seemed a logical proposal.

The two caves of Camp 1 were connected by a window hole, but because of the draught which streamed through we kept the hole blocked with a rucksack and spare clothes. Thus without thinking we had come to a conclusion without involving John, Brian and Pete. Next morning, as Ade left to go down for a rest, since now there was only room for two people at Camp 2, and he wanted to be ready to take over once the cave was dug, he poked his head into the other cave and found complete disagreement with the proposal. It seemed so logical a solution to an impasse we had now battled against for almost a fortnight that I had assumed it was in everyone's minds.

All three in the cave next door felt it was too risky to place all our hopes on finding a place suitable for digging a cave on ground no one had yet reached. Their proposal was to dig a cave at the site of Camp 2. Arguments in favour of both points of view were pushed back and forth. Nothing was lost, the bitter weather precluded any movement for a time anyway. A compromise was reached. Al and I would continue with our plan but the other three would also come up and start to dig a cave near the tents as a fall back position should the first plan prove over-ambitious. They could not stay up at Camp 2, but would dig for as long as possible before returning to Camp 1.

Next day I woke early and looked out of the cave at dawn. The sky was clear and the wind less strong. A bank of cloud low in the sky to the south seemed far enough away to present no immediate threat. We breakfasted, fastened on crampons and harness and prepared to go. The bank of cloud now filled the sky completely to the south, the front edge already catching the West Shoulder, and Nuptse's summit poured forth its own stream. Al and I looked at each other undecided and annoyed. I felt as if the mountain, like an anonymous, perverse bureaucracy, was treating us without feeling.

From the confines of their cave, Brian said he thought we should go up and Pete echoed his opinion. Their tunnelled view revealed only blue skies. Even on seeing the advancing cloud Pete was forthright in his insistence that we should go up: 'It doesn't matter if you go up and the weather turns bad. If you get worn out again at Camp 2 there are plenty of other people to replace you.'

Even had I agreed with his philosophy I resented being pushed like this into an action of which I was uncertain. Al and I wandered down away from the cave, down the upper slopes of the Rongbuk glacier into China. We wanted to wait an hour to see if the weather improved and also to gain a view of the summit which, from the caves of Camp 1, was hidden by the Western Shoulder. The slopes formed a gentle descent for half a mile before breaking up into crevasses and becoming a convoluted mass of ice towers and pinnacles where the glacier changed direction.

Across the glacier basin from where we stood we could clearly see the North Ridge, scene of many of the early attempts to climb Everest, and lost somewhere in the ice-coated immensity of the upper slopes of the mountain were the bodies of Mallory and Irvine. I felt very much the novice gazing on history. From the head of the basin rose a fine line of snow bisecting the rock of the North Face. Somewhere in that region Sherpa Ang Phu had died when he slipped whilst descending during the Yugoslav expedition to the West Ridge in 1979.

Above our Camp 2 on the West Ridge we could see that the slopes eased back and a thousand feet above the camp there was a hollow in the snow which gave hope of a possible site for a cave.

We returned to the caves of Camp 1 to find Brian retching outside. In the relentless cold of the winter he had no hope of recovering if he stayed on the mountain. He and John descended to Base Camp.

That evening on the radio Ade called us up and let us know that one member of the Japanese team had been killed when he slipped from the ice slopes below their Camp 3 on the other side of the mountain. I did not know the man in question; he was as anonymous as any fatality mentioned in a news bulletin. I felt no sense of loss as at the death of a friend, but a sickening sense of the futility of this whole enterprise of climbing, the inherent folly of the pursuit, pervaded my thoughts. We settled down to sleep that night talking about our roles as pawns in a game of our own choosing.

Al, Pete and I left next day in similar weather to that which had made us uncertain about starting the day before. The wind streamed steadily across the plateau and the slopes up to Camp 2. I was surprised to recognise in the crisp surface of the snow the marks of my crampons from the last time I had been up. My crampons were completely different from anyone else's, having a distinctive rectangular shape. In spite of all the snow which had fallen, the constant action of the wind had swept the slopes clear, preserving the imprint. At any other season more snow may fall, but the temperature is higher, the snow contains more moisture and adheres more readily to a surface, and above all the wind is neither so fierce nor so constant. I was ahead of the other two and saw one figure turn back from the start of the ropes. At Camp 2 I spent some time clearing the tent of snow, making it ready for a late return. If our plan was to work we would be climbing till nightfall and would want to just tumble into our sleeping bags on our return. Much snow had infiltrated the tent during the events surrounding the stormy evacuation of a couple of days ago. Twenty feet above the box tent lay the sad wreckage of the tent I had spent three nights in some long time ago. The platform we had laboured so hard to dig was still there, partly covered in drifted snow, through which poked tent material, abandoned rucksacks and broken tent poles.

Suddenly Pete came into view, rising over the shoulder of rock above the tents and dropping down. I had assumed it to be Al who was coming up. Pete explained that the wind had chilled Al to the point where he was worried he was getting frostbite. The prospect of five hours pulling upwards on ropes in the same wind caused him to turn back and descend to Base Camp. It was more than just feeling chilly. By this time we had been at Base Camp or above for five weeks and the punishing effect of living in such extreme cold was taking its toll. Sometimes it was too difficult to force down the unappetising food on the mountain and even at Base Camp the meals seemed to be less and less palatable. Without a big daily intake of food it was impossible to keep warm.

Al's absence was a blow. I regarded the twins as the strongest and fittest of us all, so for Al to go down was psychologically very discomforting. Pete and I made ready to climb, neither of us really knowing each other, and with that detailed politeness which characterises the interaction of strangers, we agreed upon a way of tackling the wind-scoured slopes above.

The uncertain weather of early morning had changed unnoticed into an afternoon of blue skies, sun and only light wind. I led off. The climbing was not difficult but troubled by slabs of loose snow adhering uncertainly to the underlying firmer surface I skirted round these slabs, fearing lest they give way and the accumulated might of a vast area should transform the insubstantial patches into an overwhelming, deadly wave. I led for 300 feet, stopping frequently to rest and, when Pete took over, relaxed in the enjoyment of a rare, fine day. For the first time I was actually enjoying being on the mountain; the view north into the brown, mysterious land of Tibet, the receding rows of hills to north and south, their contours etched more beautifully by the sinking sun, all filled me with a suppressed sense of privilege and, exaltation. Unfortunately it was an enjoyment I could not share, for Pete was far above me. Much of climbing on a big mountain is solitary, many hours are passed in the sole company of one's own shadow, other people separated by distance or weather from communication.

I wanted the afternoon to go on and on. I wished that everyone else could share the experience, for this if anything would revive the flagging spirit of the expedition.

When Pete had fixed 300 feet of rope in place I took another turn and took a false line up a runnel of snow beside an area of glassy ice. Pete corrected the error by traversing beneath the ice, and we lost some time in sorting out the ropes. He disappeared round a ridge of snow, and when the rope stopped moving I followed.

Nothing prepared me for what I saw when I came round the ridge. My attention was on the rope and on my crampons trying to find purchase on an icy passage. The slope had eased back completely now and I was almost walking. Looking up I was halted by the towering sight of the summit pyramid of Everest, looming up so close, reddening in the setting sun which threw into relief all the cracks and wrinkles of this ageless mountain. I looked and looked as the colours changed, the red deepened, and dark shadow crept inexorably upward finally to wipe all colour away. Pete shared his thoughts with a brief: 'Great isn't it?' and we made ready to return to Camp 2, well pleased with the day.

The unexpected sight made such an impression on me that I slid down the ropes, bubbling with eagerness to radio down the news of our progress. I tried a call at 5.30 p.m. before reaching the Camp but had no success and my numb, clumsy hands, cramped by the post-sunset chill, made me fear to use the radio lest I dropped it. It was a mere half hour back to the tent compared with the whole afternoon we had spent climbing upwards.

When we did make contact at the pre-arranged fallback time

of 6 p.m. I transmitted the satisfaction both of us felt at breaking through the impasse we had reached at Camp 2 and our enthusiasm inspired by the sight we had seen. Ade, at Base Camp, was surprised. They had had a cold, windy day below and had expected us to fare worse. He promised to come up next day with Paul and Alan.

The satisfaction at the day's work and the conviction that we would be able to get a snow cave above helped us face the prospect of a grim night in the coffin of a tent which remained standing at Camp 2. The box tent was only just big enough for two of us. No movement could be made without the cooperation of the other person. Pete drew himself up into a corner of the tent to make room for me to cook. I had explained to him the great disinclination I feel to wake up on a morning and that if it suited him I would cook all the evening meal if he would cook the breakfast. Since there was only room for one person to cook at a time this made a logical division of work. For the next three hours I melted snow, made a stew, made drinks and passed them over.

'I'm glad you like plenty to drink,' said Pete. 'I was with Brian and he preferred to go to sleep rather than eat and drink.' Pete was acquiring a reputation for being a big eater, maintaining a capacity to funnel food down endlessly. On an expedition it is an admirable accomplishment as normally everyone loses weight due to the loss of appetite, with the consequent diminishment of strength and stamina. In spite of the value of being able to continue eating, Pete's ability to do so did arouse a sense of annoyance and envy. It was irrational, but part of the inevitable dynamics of a living situation where comfort is at a minimum and sensitivity close to the surface.

It was so uncomfortable in the tent that there was little hope of dropping off to sleep. We each took a sedative and dozed fitfully. I was half aware of Pete being restless and muffled groans escaped from him each time he moved. At midnight I did not feel as if I had slept at all and when I spoke to Pete he said he could not sleep either because of some pains in his side. We took a sleeping pill each and I took two headache tablets. It was a heavy dosage and I woke at dawn dazed and groggy. Pete, unaccountably, was wide awake. He prepared breakfast and I trailed unenthusiastically after him to the top of the ropes, our high point of the previous day.

There was no need to fix rope on the ground we had reached as it was only gently sloping, and the weather had remained unusually calm for a second day. We did run out some rope, however, until we arrived at a bank of snow in which we intended to dig a snow cave. Without the guideline of a rope it could be impossible to find the cave in a blizzard or hold on against a wind.

My head had cleared of its earlier muzziness. Pete, smaller than me but more stocky, disguised in a similar spaceman's garb of quilted red suit, plodded up steadily. He had a purposeful pace; I projected on to him the assumption that he was unaffected by the debility which I felt. Even walking close together little was said. I was panting hard and any comment I made sounded as if I attached great weight to it after much deliberation; in reality I was pausing to catch my breath between each word.

We started digging into a bank of snow, steeper than the slope we had climbed, intending to burrow horizontally into the hillside in a narrow tunnel before making a larger cavern. The site was some incalculable distance below the crest of the West Shoulder. Pete thought it to be only a short distance; I thought it would take at least an hour to climb. I am not sure if it is an effect of altitude or simply lack of objects by which to estimate scale, but gauging distance is a difficult and often disappointing exercise on a mountain.

Ten minutes of digging was enough to tire us, so we took it in turns. The snow was perfect for excavation. Unlike the Eskimos, who have dozens of words for snow, our language is limited. If there was a word to describe the ideal snow for a snow cave, it would have applied to the snow we were digging, firm without being icy. I took a turn, kneeling in the deepening shaft we now had running into the hillside, the white snow of the surface turning blue in the inner recesses of the shaft with the diffusion of light through it. I noticed a black mark at the end of the tunnel which by this time was six feet deep. Suspecting a rock, which would render our efforts futile, I struck at it and the snow around gave way to reveal a dark hole. At first I recoiled in shock, but when nothing more happened I crawled forward and stared down into a gaping crevasse, totally enclosed with a roof of ice and festooned inside with fantastic formations of crystalline ice and blocks of snow, a winter wonderland. Some huge blocks spanned the crevasse, forming a shelf; to the left the hole dropped away into bottomless blackness. I withdrew in awe and motioned Pete to look in.

Crevasses have connotations of terror for a mountaineer and my first instinct was to start afresh elsewhere. Pete was similarly nonplussed. If it was sensible to use the crevasse as a shelter it would save us two days of excavation, but if it was unstable we could wake up to a slow death from suffocation or a plunge into a newly opened chasm.

We decided to enter the crevasse and examine from inside its potential. We kept the rope fastened to our waists and tied to some stakes driven firmly into the snow outside, a lifeline to safety. I dropped inside on to the shelf, feeling as if I was entering forbidden territory, with the nervousness of a burglar on his first job. We took up separate stances and flailed away with ice axes at the ice formations hanging from the roof. The roof was only a couple of feet thick in parts and a blue, suffused light penetrating the snow illuminated the interior. We used the snow knocked down from the ceiling to level the floor, and as we grew more at home in this icy fairyland I crawled to the furthest end in one direction where the cave funnelled down to a cone, and the bright light showed that the roof was thinnest. I knocked down with a sense of regret the weird, fantastical formations, widening the cave. Pete worked on making a new entrance as the hole we had dropped in through was eight feet above the floor. After a couple of hours, completely at ease in this pit now, we had enlarged the cave sufficiently for three people to sleep inside, with plenty more space that could be easily cleared. We were well pleased with our work; in a matter of hours we had ready a cave which we had thought would take days to prepare, and in two days we had broken through the psychological barrier which had surrounded Camp 2.

When we came to leave we had difficulty escaping. Pete, tunnelling away to make a new entrance, had been doing so directly below the hole by which we had entered. There was fifteen feet of snow to dig through and he had only partially completed it. Thus, there was a gaping cavity and nothing on which to stand to reach the upper hole. I struggled and berated Pete before managing to claw my way out. Pete similarly struggled, much to my satisfaction.

We had let ourselves have an easier day now that we had achieved our objective. We reached the tent at Camp 2 comfortably before dark and transmitted the happy news of our fortunate discovery. Pete and I intended to ferry all our gear up from Camp 2 to the snow cave, Camp 3, next day, before going down for a rest.

The radio call brought bad news. Wan Chup, the cook, was critically ill and Pete was asked to consider going down in his capacity as doctor. He had the symptoms described to him over the radio, vomiting, delirium and excretion of blood. Pete guessed at a perforated ulcer. The doctor from the Italian camp had come over, but if there was no improvement Pete resigned himself to descending next morning.

It had always been a *bête noire* of Pete's, that just such a conflict would arise between his responsibility as a doctor and his wishes as a climber. There was no other option, Wan Chup did seem seriously ill, and although Pete was the first to acknowledge that doctors cannot wave magic wands, if Wan Chup died the whole expedition would be stigmatised for its irresponsibility if it was known that the doctor was out of reach on the mountain.

Pete's face wore a look of glumness for the rest of the evening. I agreed that his first responsibility was to descend, but I regretted to see him go. This had been the first time I had had anything to do with him on the expedition and I had come to realise that the anonymous person who kept in the background, who had not seemed to be going as strongly as some, was in fact driven by a purposeful determination. Perhaps he had been overshadowed by the extrovert garrulousness of some of us or was simply pacing himself until he had found his own level. Whatever the explanation, I was now impressed at the new person I had seen emerge in the last couple of days. There was every reason for all of us to be mystified by Pete. He seemed genuinely to enjoy being on his own, often walking for hours at a time far from the company of anyone. Before we reached Base Camp he sometimes went off on a solo sortie, soaking up new sights without needing to share the experience. On the mountain we had grown accustomed to his eccentric tendency to set off late and often arrive so late that we came to call him the Midnight Cowboy.

I felt a fraud beside him. Suddenly on returning to the tent I was overcome with fatigue but, obliged by the pact of my own instigation on the cooking of meals; I had to prepare the food. I spent the next three hours melting snow and making drinks and meals. These I passed to a reclining Pete who seemed unaffected by the exertions of the last two days and devoured everything I gave him. After heating the water for the main meal, I realised that I could not face eating it, so I handed a huge panful of lasagne to Pete. I had the useless satisfaction of seeing him for the first time unable to finish a meal.

Another squashed and restless night passed, worse than the last, listening to Pete's groans, to the wind outside and finally capitulating to the recurring temptation to take a sedative in the search for sleep.

Pete gave me a brew of tea before leaving in the morning. An earlier than usual radio call told him of the anxious vigil kept beside Wan Chup's feverish bed by the members down below. Reluctantly he left and I dropped off to sleep, now that I was no longer constricted. I woke at midday with a clear head and hurried to ready myself before Ade arrived and caught me still in bed.

It was 1 p.m. when he reached the tent on his way to the cave above. I had a warm drink ready for him but he still mocked my idleness. He continued on to the cave and I followed, glad at the thought that I would be spending no more nights in that tent. As I toiled, heavy laden, up the same slopes for the third day running, the snow turned pink with the setting sun. Far below, a red matchstick man appeared by the tent of Camp 2. It was Paul on his way up, but it would be dark before he reached the cave.

Paul had stopped off at Camp 2 and added even more weight to his monstrous, heavy load. His familiar hearty laugh had something of a chagrined resignation to it now. Ade gave out news of the air of discouragement which was hanging over Base Camp. It was the middle of January and the feeling was that the attempt to climb the West Ridge was turning into a war of attrition which was taking a heavy toll. There had been discussion about fixing a date in early February for the porters to arrive and for us to leave Base Camp if we were not in striking distance of the summit.

This was demoralising news, especially so in contrast to the euphoria of the progress of the last few days. If only everyone could have a couple of perfect days on the mountain such as Pete and I had experienced, attitudes would change and morale would be restored.

The cave at Camp 3 was spacious, and consequently much colder than Camp 1. A constant draught streamed up, seemingly from the bowels of the mountain, through the black hole at the far end of the cave. Paul, for all his fatigue, could not eat much as he had developed an aversion to the freeze-dried food we had and which was the mainstay of our diet. It was an unpleasant night, the three of us huddled together, unembarrassed, to share our bodily warmth.

At night we slept totally enclosed in our sleeping bags, still wearing every bit of clothing except boots. The hood of the sleeping bags could be drawn closed round the head, leaving only a small hole for ventilation. We woke each morning to an icy layer surrounding the hole, formed as breath condensed and froze to the outer surface of the bag.

By luck the cave at Camp 3 was in the lee of the West Ridge, sometimes gaining protection from the wind. On the morning after our first night in the cave, Paul volunteered to spend the day improving the accommodation and digging the new entrance. Pete's excavations were still unfinished and entry to or exit from the cave still necessitated negotiating an eight-foot drop. Paul's task was to burrow through fifteen feet of snow outwards from the floor level of the cave and to block in the first entrance.

I felt that Ade and I had the more desirable option; we set off to reach the West Shoulder, to investigate the route along the crest of the ridge to Camp 4. Words do not emanate of themselves the slowness, of movement, the lassitude at such heights; memory cheats and passes over the blank spaces between events; half an hour to put on boots and then strap on crampons sounds ridiculous but is normal. Life on this mountain was a slow-motion actuality.

We were ready to leave, hovering on the outside of the cave; the momentary hesitation before breaking new ground, the slight reluctance too first. Ade pulled out his bar of chocolate-coated mint cake: 'Should give me energy,' he said. 'I need it.' It sounded a good idea, though I was not a follower of the Burgess devotion to diet control and energy foods. I ate a few squares and Ade swallowed all his. 'You've not eaten a whole bar, have you?' I was incredulous at his capacity to consume so much of the same sickly sweetmeat at one go. 'I need it to get up there,' he laughed, intrigued by my astonishment, and he strode off powerfully upwards as if to make his point.

The snow was firm and the crampons held securely. Crack lines crossed the surface and we came upon an area of larger crevasses. At any other season these would have been worrying illustrations of the lethal mobility of the slope, but one of the few advantages of winter was proving to be that movement of the snow, as well as of humans, was, if not stopped completely, considerably slowed down. We were reasonably sure that there was no danger of avalanche.

Sparkling streamers of snow came whirling over the West Shoulder as we neared the crest and climbed into the wind. Ade was a distance ahead and, unwilling to capitulate to his credence in diet-determining performance, I busied myself taking photographs of his silhouette against the rising sun, thus disguising my slower pace.

We carried ropes and snow stakes, but were not using the ropes for the moment. Though icy, the angle of the slope was easy. A slip could mean a fatal, uncontrollable 5,000-foot slide but this was our medium; this was the everyday routine of a mountaineer as familiar or dangerous as driving a car. The growing wind, tugging at my body, heightened my concentration; in my hand was an ice axe, a third support, held ready to drive into the ice to arrest any fall. The silhouette above disappeared over the crest of the ridge. I could not hurry to catch up; I could only continue at the same steady pace, frequently halting, and enjoying the sight of Pumori, which towers above Base Camp, dropping away below.

Ade was sitting on a lone rock protruding from a rounded plateau of wind-hardened snow, bending now against the force of the wind. There was probably a smile on his face but ice masked his mouth and goggles concealed his eyes. Behind him a huge panorama unfolded – the walls of Everest, Lhotse and Nuptse formed an arc round the deep basin of the Western Cwm, one of the forbidden places of the earth. The Cwm is the valley leading to these mountains, the entrance to which is guarded by the formidable Khumbu Icefall. We were surrounded now by mountains, snowy ranks receding into the distance on every side. A few years ago I would have found the sight appalling, so many mountains to climb, so much suffering to reach their summits, so much effort needed and so many doubts about my own ability and resolve. Now I had come to know that I would not stop climbing; this mountain scene was exhilarating rather than oppressive, full of endless opportunity. Sometimes I feel as if mountains have become an addiction, the pleasure gone, the compulsion to partake remaining. Rarely blessed with the enjoyment of the moment, I had come to realise the satisfaction of going to the limit, physically and mentally, of dipping into danger and exhaustion, of returning full of enthusiasm for life and appreciation for every part of existence.

My feet trudged on over the humps of the plateau. Ade said he was feeling the altitude but I pressed him to go further. The plateau narrowed to a ridge, the ridge reared up, a knife-edge of snow running into the summit pyramid which now looked close. To our right the slope fell away steeply, 3,000 feet to the bottom of the Cwm. I was tired too. Only the desire to reach the Shoulder and see a new panorama, after weeks on the slopes below, had driven me up. Ever-cautious, Ade was wary of going too far along the ridge. The wind was gusting strongly; if it gained more strength it could easily pick us up and throw us over the ridge or drop us into the Western Cwm. We agreed on a point to reach before turning back, but we had been looking at different points, and when the ridge steepened to an angle where it would have been foolish to continue without ropes, Ade suggested that we had come far enough for the day.

We had reached 24,000 feet. The remainder of the ridge looked more difficult but providing the wind was not too strong we should be able to reach a site for Camp 4. It would have to be another cave, gruelling as its excavation might be, at 25,000 feet. Beyond, that a ramp of snow cut diagonally leftwards, into the North Face to a narrow gully slicing the vast yellow rock area of Everest's summit pyramid. That was the last major obstacle. We fastened our sacks of gear to a stake driven into the snow and turned back, well pleased.

We descended to Camp 3, pilgrims returning from some holy shrine. The distance we had covered was vast and descending required total concentration, but we were back with Paul before the afternoon was far gone.

The new entrance was ready, the old one sealed with blocks of snow, but light came through this thinner layer and through chinks between the blocks. The cave inside was illuminated as by the patterned windows of a clerestory.

Alan flopped into the cave unannounced at the end of the afternoon. We had not established satisfactory radio communication yet from Camp 3 so we were uncertain about the movements of anyone else on the mountain. Alan let us know that John was due to arrive at the Lho La that afternoon and should be on his way to Camp 3 the next day.

Paul had hardly eaten since he had arrived. A drink and some soup was all that he could manage. He was apologetic, seeing this inadequacy as detrimental to his own strength and therefore the strength of the team. It was a little more uncomfortable with four of us; there was plenty of room, we were utilising perhaps only one-third of the cave, but only this third was widened and levelled for use. At the far end was the bottomless pit which we would never fill but which provided us with the luxury of an indoor toilet.

Alan had the worst position, at the edge of the levelled area, using rucksacks to increase his sleeping space. Paul and Ade in the middle were warmest, sheltered from the draught by warm bodies on every side.

I was ready to go down next day, in need of a rest and making way for replacements. Paul felt he should descend as well, being too weak from lack of food to be capable of going further. Ade was listless after three days' continuous movement upwards. He intended to rest for a day before going up again. Only Alan was keen to do something positive; if nothing else he would descend to the now redundant Camp 2 and ferry up the remaining gear.

Alan crawled out through the tunnel and came back with the disheartening news that it was blowing a gale outside and snowing. He disappeared again after a while and when he did not return we presumed him to have gone to Camp 2. Paul made ready to go down, voicing his misgivings and expressing his anxiety that he might be obliged to return to Britain if the expedition was to go on much longer. He had given an optimistic forecast of his return as being the middle of January. It was now 18 January and if we went on it would be the middle of February before we got back. Paul was a college lecturer and had a more rigid timetable than most of us.

Rather than leave Ade without the certainty of a partner, I decided to stay on another night. We passed the day eating and drinking as often as the motivation allowed. Night came without the return of Alan or the arrival of John. Spindrift had been blowing into the cave and we sealed off the entrance with rucksacks.

Although we could receive some radio transmissions, we were not in line of sight with Base Camp and our messages were not getting through. It takes a stronger signal to transmit than to receive and after several tries Ade gave up, though even from inside the cave we could sometimes hear the calls from Base. Al's flat voice came weakly over the air: 'Base to Lho La and Camp 2 or 3 do you read me?' repeated over and over. 'In case you are listening ... ' the words trailed on lost in the crackle of interference.

'Just listen to our kid's voice,' complained Ade in disgust. 'If he put some expression into it we might be able to pick something up. He's just droning away.'

There was an uneasy feeling about the way things were going. I was not much use at the moment. I had been on the mountain for ten days and knew I needed a rest if I was going to contribute anything more. The question was growing whether Everest really was too difficult in winter. Certainly the cold was more insupportable, sleep was difficult and headaches were more frequent than usual. Even inside a down suit and a sleeping bag feet were nearly always chilled. On eating a meal, warmth could be felt percolating down to the toes as combustion of the food took place. As a topic of conversation this often replaced the weather in its popularity.

The Burgesses have the disadvantage of being unable to sleep on their sides. Alan put forward the explanation as being the width of their shoulders, no pillows being high enough to support their heads. Whatever the reason, Ade was forced to lie on his back, facing upwards to a ceiling, a couple of feet above him, which was festooned with 'long, gangly, white fronds', as he described them. Each time he coughed, a shower of these fronds descended, dislodged by the slightest movement of air. The cave was anyway filled with the fine particles of snow driven in by the wind through any crevice. A torch beam would lance through the air, catching the floating particles in its light like a beam from the lamp of a bus in a London fog. In one wall of the cave was an unsuspected crack to the outside through which fine snow was pouring. It was the worst night yet in a cave.

Powder snow covered everything when we woke. A dim light filtered into the cave; there was no sound of the wind. There was no increase in warmth with the morning, the thermometer showing a steady -20 degrees Celsius. I put some lumps of snow into a pan and lay back waiting for it to melt.

Two hours later I prepared to go down to Camp 2 to clear it of any remaining gear. Ade needed to rest further. I pulled aside the rucksacks blocking the exit. A small shaft remained of our tunnel; the rest was filled for fifteen feet with snow. At the far end of the shaft sunlight caught the snow. The storm was over but we were snowed in.

When I dug the tunnel clear and popped through to the outside it was still blustery, but there were clearings in the sky, and the force of the storm was spent. A new, crisp whiteness coated the mountainside and the ropes leading down were buried.

I ferried up more sleeping bags and food from Camp 2, and brought the ruined tent to use as a curtain on our tunnel. Gradually we were improving our living quarters.

No one else arrived that day and with little remaining reserves of strength after eleven days on the mountain I resolved to descend next day. Ade too was tired and he came down. Deep banks of snow covered the slopes, and our steps dislodged these, precipitating small avalanches. It was better that we should do this than wait for a dangerous accumulation to form and an overwhelming avalanche to sweep down of its own volition. The wind was constant but not too strong. I was stumbling, but it was from fatigue rather than the wind.

Near the bottom a lone figure was coming upwards. It was John, distinguishable by the colour of his clothes. He was covered in snow from pulling clear the ropes and caked blood from some unmentioned mishap was mingled with the ice on his face when we met him. With the lack of radio communication we had come to an awkward imbalance of movement on the mountain. John, on his own, would be able to achieve little at Camp 3 and I did not envy him his lone vigil up there till someone from below should join him.

John had been at Camp 1 on the night of the most recent storm and he had a woeful tale of waking to find that he too was snowed in. Desperate to relieve himself, he had done so into a plastic bag and disposed of it hours later when he had finally dug himself free.

Troubled with doubts about the present situation on the mountain, we left John moving upwards and ourselves trailed on to Base Camp.

Enthusiasm at the progress we had to report was tempered by the general gloom about our chances of success. There had been more sickness in the camp. At our instigation Brian, Pete and Al went up, in spite of ominous weather signs, to the Lho La and we entered a period of discussion at Base Camp about tactics and our prospects.

By afternoon it was snowing steadily. We were anticipating the arrival of the mail runner but had doubts about the likelihood of his bringing any mail. Two Sherpas, however, arrived first, one of them, Nima Norbu, being our new Sirdar to replace Dawa. He brought unwelcome news of knee-deep snow down at Syangboche and the unlikelihood of flights into the airstrip for many days.

Base Camp was no longer a comfortable place. Since before Christmas we had had few spells of fine weather. The tents sagged under the weight of snow, and even if a day started clear, clouds usually enveloped the sky before it was out and the camp was little more than a bleak, chill wasteland. I began to prefer the idea of being back on the mountain – at least there I expected to be uncomfortable, to have to struggle to survive. I felt cheated here and annoyed when I found that at every moment of the day I was conscious of being cold.

A scrapyard of blackened, useless stoves lay outside the cook tent. One by one our stoves, paraffin and petrol alike, had packed up under the extremes of winter, fourteen stoves in all. Alan and Brian had gone on, a borrowing mission to the Japanese camp and returned with two enormous paraffin stoves which we hoped would last us for the rest of the expedition.

The Japanese equally were stalled by the conditions on the mountain. As well as being shaken by the death of one of their members, several others of the climbers and five Sherpas were frostbitten. Some of the Japanese displayed on their cheeks and noses the tell-tale purple weals of once-frozen flesh; one of the Sherpas was going to need part of his foot amputating and another some fingers. A train of yaks had been summoned, to carry them down to the airstrip, and hospital.

On 20 January three Japanese had left their Base Camp to go

back up for one final attempt. The Italians, attempting Lhotse, had not made much progress beyond the trail which they shared with the Japanese to the foot of their mountain. From the start they had seemed lost in the face of their objective, with clothing and tentage hardly different from what they would use in the Alps. They too, were running out of steam.

The only way to obtain a semblance of warmth was to sit in a tent, when the sun was out, with the doors zipped closed to exclude the breeze. The heat of the sun on the tent walls raised the temperature inside to a luxurious degree and, though the sociable atmosphere of the dining tent was better than solitude, the rare opportunity of restoring circulation was too good to miss.

I lay there one day enjoying the solar heating and the glowing feel of warmth returning to my feet, thinking over events. At 7 a.m. I had listened in to Ade making the radio call to the Lho La. The sky had been unsettled but held the promise of clearing. His brother was exhausted after breaking trail for several hours up to the Lho La. The walls and slabs of rock were much changed from when we had first climbed them. Snow a foot deep concealed footholds and left the hands numb from groping through it to find purchase. The journey to Camp 1 took twice as long. Brian had had a bad night and did not feel like moving. Ade exhorted his brother to persuade Pete to go on up to Camp 3 where John, from whom we had heard nothing since passing him on the way up, was still alone.

By 9 a.m. the sky was really overcast and on a second, prearranged radio call, Ade was told that the weather on the Lho La was atrocious but Pete had left nevertheless to relieve the beleaguered John. It was good news – at least there was some activity.

From the experience of reaching the West Shoulder I was convinced that given good weather we could climb this mountain. The Shoulder is at a height of approximately 24,000 feet and it had felt similarly bad to 24,000 feet on any other mountain at other times of the year. The main difference was the force of the wind, the deadly cold and the rapidity with which the weather could change. 'If only the weather would hold,' I wrote in my diary.

'I won't mind the suffering involved; I do not think that the cold plus lack of oxygen plus dry air will be what will stop us.'

This sort of expedition was not something to become addicted to and subconsciously the conviction had formed that if we should get up Everest this time I would not come again to the Himalayas in winter. I wrote further: 'I suppose I have always connected mountaineering at its limit with arduous, almost unbelievable hardship, for our generation this is it – the Himalayas in winter, when a few short hours of warmth are all one can expect, if lucky'.

A commotion outside heralded the arrival of Mingma, our cook boy, who was now acting as mail runner. In spite of the lack of flights he had some mail to offer; residue from a previous flight or brought by some other mysterious route we could not fathom. Disappointingly, there was no newspaper. We were all together in the dining tent, Graham rocking back and forth on his feet trying to encourage the circulation, the brief sun of midday now concealed behind grey clouds.

Ade and I had been insistent, on coming back to Base Camp from Camp 3, that there should be people on the mountain at each of the camps all the time, and that if the weather was bad they should stick it out ready to push the route further or move up to relieve those at the front. These ideas came out of our own experience of waiting for support and seeing John going up on his own with no back-up. But the continuing hostile weather, and now the news that Pete was forcing his way up to Camp 3 in a storm, was taken as a rebuttal of this suggestion.

Alan advocated waiting until the weather did clear and then having everyone move on the mountain together in the hope of doing eight man-days of work instead of two with the rotation system.

We had reached 23 January. Our permission for Everest was due to expire on the 31st of the month. Alan had used the Japanese radio connection with Kathmandu to ask for an extension of our permit. We were granted an extra two weeks.

Food and fuel were running short and our diet had become very monotonous. The question of arranging a date for departure arose once again. Still enthusing from the positive progress I had been involved in, I argued against any suggestion of fixing a date for departure: 'If we state that we will leave by a certain date, we will have already decided on the outcome of the expedition.'

Psychologically we will have given up. We should not be thinking of how efficiently we can leave, but of continuing, if there is a chance of getting up the mountain, even after our permit has run out.

Alan pointed out that such an action would inevitably alienate the government of Nepal, since in the past they had reacted strongly against anyone breaking their rules.

'Climbing is all about breaking rules. It's in the nature of the game. Would the North Face of the Eiger ever have been climbed if the climbers of the day had abided by the laws laid down forbidding any attempt on it? We should think of extending the permission again, sending down for more food and fuel, not letting their lack dictate our movements.'

As official leader, Alan was in an invidious position. Any one of the rest of us could do as he wished, break any number of laws, but the responsibility lay with the leader and the sanction most often enforced is to ban the leader from Nepal for a number of years. For a keen climber this was anathema, especially if the punishment was enforced for an action of someone other than himself.

Basically there was agreement that at some stage we would have to make a decision about leaving; we could not stay forever. Alan and Brian, as the two who shouldered most of the burden of organisation, wanted to have considered the practicalities and time-scales involved in departing from the mountain. It was agreed that a certain amount of good weather was necessary for success and that by the end of the month we would have a clear idea of the likely outcome. Allen Jewhurst volunteered to stay behind as long as need be in Kathmandu to clear up any formalities and forward the gear if this would set minds at rest regarding delays in getting home.

The discussion cleared the air. There was a renewed sense of commitment to stick it out to the end. Photographs, maps and books were pored over and passed round to glean every bit of information and encouragement. The contours of the summit pyramid were compared on the map with those of other known areas of the mountain, and the final chapters of the book by Hornbein and Unsoeld on their ascent of Everest, triumphing at the eleventh hour against all the odds, were taken as an example.

Conversation drifted down from the intense level of the afternoon and by evening, after an unsuccessful radio call at 6 p.m., we were given to musing on more light-hearted subjects. The abominable snowman entered the conversation and its existence on Everest, as reported by the Japanese, given as a reason for the lack of communication from those at Camp 1 on the Lho La.

Alan developed on this theme and went off into a wild fantasy about Pete and his ferocious appetite, sketching out a scenario of the climbers who vanish one by one, from the Lho La with only Pete surviving, growing fatter and fatter, to be last seen making off down the Rongbuk glacier. Ade summed up the erosion of our senses after so long in the mountains as he tried to make out a list of basic equipment needed for his next expedition. When, after an hour of pondering, he had only three items on his list, he looked up with a puzzled expression and said:

'It's hard to think, after a few weeks here, isn't it?'

10 ATTRITION AND THE TURNING POINT

24 January dawned snowy and dull. Depression seemed to hang above and below. However, radio communications were at last effective. Pete had taken up with him some wire with which he had rigged up an extension aerial and the same had been done at the Lho La. Communications could now be conducted from the comfort of the sleeping bags inside the caves.

There was no progress above Camp 3. John had been hit by a return of amoebic dysentery and was trying to nurture his strength to descend. Brian and Al lower down at Camp 1 had attempted to go on up to Camp 3 but had had to retreat after being battered and tossed about by the winds.

Paul and Alan were ready to go up on to the mountain but whilst no progress was possible for anyone up there they stayed at Base Camp where the energy drain was less. Paul had misgivings about voicing the need for his return home, not wanting to undermine the momentum of the trip. He stated briefly and clearly why he would have to leave, intending by so doing to put his case and then let it be forgotten. He was going up one more time, knowing that there was no possibility of his reaching the summit in the time left, but meaning to help the expedition for as long as he could.

Maurizio, the lone Italian at their Base Camp, frequently visited us in his search for company. He was not a climber but had come with the expedition to act as interpreter. The rest of his friends were at Camp 2 in the Western Cwm, his only contact with them for many days being by radio. True to style, the Italian cuisine was enlivened with blocks of parmesan cheese, hunks of ham and other long-forgotten delicacies. By one means or another Brian, a ruthless negotiator, had managed to strike an extraordinary bargain by which we obtained a selection of these in exchange for some of the freeze-dried food for the mountain, of which we had an abundance and for which most of us by now had acquired a hearty aversion. For a time the much loathed 'noodle stew', to which we had been reduced, was kept at bay.

The Japanese encampment had an air of gloom too. We were always welcome and for a change of scene one or two people would pay them a visit from time to time. The visits had grown more frequent in an endeavour to obtain a more accurate assessment of the weather. They had their 'facsimile' machine which reproduced a weather map transmitted from Delhi. And received a weather report by radio from Kathmandu from a team member who had returned there to sort out formalities after the death of one of their group.

The map and reports bore little relation to the mountains by which we were surrounded. Such convoluted terrain creates its own weather and all we could look for from the broadcast information was a general trend. On 24 January the Japanese informed us that the information they had received was that it was impossible to make any predictions for the next week. The weather map was a mass of tightly packed lines covering the whole Indian sub-continent.

The members of their own team were stuck at Camp 2. They had tried to make progress to Camp 3 and up to the South Col but had been forced back by wind and poor visibility. Now their food was running very low. They could not descend to Base Camp because the route through the icefall had been destroyed with the collapse of several walls of ice, ruining the bridges across crevasses which they had so laboriously built. A repair party from below would have to go up first to replace the ladders.

There was a set of bathroom scales at the Japanese camp and we weighed ourselves. Alan and Graham had lost two stones. They were both gaunt, lean figures compared to their normal appearance. All of us believed we had lost weight but found there was little or no variation from our normal weights. Ade found he had put on weight, a discovery which made him feel much better.

A hurricane roared all night over the Lho La. I lay in the comfort and security of my Base Camp tent listening uneasily, aware of the demoralising effect the wind would have on Al and Brian in the cave of Camp 1. The 'mortar bomb simulation' would be pounding all night. Later in the day an apologetic Al and Brian arrived back, justifying their departure from Camp 1 by describing the debilitating effect, physically and mentally, of lying for day after day in the ice cave, waiting for the weather to improve. They felt themselves losing strength all the while and had decided to come down.

The wind did not touch us at Base Camp but just after sunset a roar which was not the wind had brought us rushing from the dining tent to see, vague and formless in the twilight, a billowing cloud of avalanche debris pouring out of the 'Burgess couloir'. One of the ice cliffs at the edge of the Lho La had collapsed. A grey, seething wall of snow advanced imperceptibly, menacingly towards the camp. Outlying streamers flung a dusting of powder snow over us and our tents, but the main mass passed by, its force largely spent in its journey of over a mile. Ade had a wry grin on his face when we had settled back into the tent.

After dark a very wasted and weary-looking John pushed his way into the dining tent. He spoke of the horror of life at Camp 3 during the storms, of the cold and the snow which forced itself in through every tiny crevice and the subsequent maelstrom of whirling snow inside. He had become very weak from dysentery and had had no option but to descend, sorry himself not to have gone further and leaving behind a disappointed Pete who was equally unable to make any progress on his own. John's experience at Camp 3 had been quite an ordeal, culminating, as he describes it himself, in a disturbed night and harrowing descent:

> The night in the cave was one long groan. The cold penetrated deep into my bones. Sleep was impossible. The moment I dozed off, my breathing became fitful and irregular. I would open my eyes, gasping

for air in the frozen, roaring blackness. At first I felt unutterably fatigued.

By 11 a.m. I knew I had to descend. Diarrhoea had returned, and through coughing so much I had developed a severe pain in my chest. I was worried that pneumonia might set in.

Outside, the weather was bad but no worse than on the days I had hauled loads up from Camp 2. Pete, keen to go on, was disappointed at my decision to go down, but he knew I had no choice. I fell over frequently as I tried to make ready to descend.

Getting down the ropes was a nightmare. The wind blew me over unexpectedly from one direction and then the other. I was attached to the rope at all times, but once I heard an unmistakable 'click', just as I was about to launch off down the rock barrier, as the karabiner which fastened my harness to the rope came unclipped. Without emotion I re-secured it and continued.

I was only halfway down when my diarrhoea overcame me, adding to my suffering. I could not stop. When I reached the Lho La the wind was too strong for me to walk. I crawled the half mile back to the caves, still being blown over by the wind and bouncing along like a ball. My cherished hope was that someone would be waiting for me at Camp 1 with a mug of tea ready, but the caves were empty. I dug the snow from the entrance before crawling in and beginning the ignominious task of cleaning myself up.

I still felt extremely ill and decided to continue the descent, lest I should be unable to do so next day if I stayed.

Only when I reached the rocks at the start of the descent did I become aware of the time. I had no strength to hurry, but forced myself down in a slow, dazed routine, checking and rechecking before I made a move. I reached the glacier at dusk.

'Not long now,' I reassured myself, relaxing slightly as I switched on my head torch. But where I had expected to find a familiar trail there was only soft, deep snow and avalanche debris. Soon it was completely dark and the light from my torch began to fail. Unfamiliar ice towers appeared all round and I sank through the soft snow at every second step, expecting each time to find the blackness of a crevasse rushing up towards me. I was lost, and the only solution was to retrace my steps and find somewhere to spend the night out.

Adrenalin kept me going and I had almost regained the edge of the glacier when I caught sight in the distance of the light of someone moving about at Base Camp. Relief penetrated my exhaustion and I trudged in the direction of the light. New snow obscured all tracks, but I knew the way now. I wondered if I would recover strength to go up again. There was the noise of chatter from the dining tent, I entered and the bright light and warmth hit me like the memory of a lost world.

John could stomach no food and retired to his tent early. It was sickening to wake to a fine day on 26 January. This was the first fine day for some time and there would be no progress still. Alan and Paul left to re-occupy Camp 1.

Late in the afternoon we caught sight of Paul through the telephoto lens nearing the top of the steep corner. He and Alan had been delayed by the deep snow which still covered the route and when there was no reply to the radio call at 6 p.m. it was an indication that they would probably be too tired next day to go on up to Camp 3. Towards evening the clouds blew up swiftly from the south.

The plan was for Ade and myself to go up the next day, hoping to occupy Camp 1 as Paul and Alan went on up to Camp 3, and for us to wait there until we could move up to replace them after they had pushed the route further and retired for a rest. Pete was also up at Camp 3, but he would be in need of a rest after being stranded there for several days through some bad storms. The basic business of survival in such cold and at such altitudes is a trying ordeal.

John was the other person who had a formal job to return to by a certain date. However, he dismissed such anxieties as he felt and resigned himself to the prospect of finding he had no job left on his return. He wanted to stay till the end.

As Ade and I left next morning to go back on to the mountain I called by John's tent to see how he was.

'Much better thanks Joe, I should be able to get back up there the day after tomorrow.'

Relieved at John's recovery, Ade and I set off, Ade at his usual steady rhythm with me panting behind. He even tempted me up the quicker route of the 'Burgess Couloir', reasoning that any loose stuff would, have been dislodged by the cataclysmic avalanche of two days ago.

As we reached the steep walls of the corner, Pete came into view, sliding swiftly down the ropes. Pete always seemed to be carrying a sack with something in it. Most of us tried to conserve energy and in descent carry nothing at all. For whatever reason, possibly to make sure that he always had extra clothing to hand, Pete's sack usually looked full.

He was reluctant to be going down, he said, but he had broken a rib. There had been no accident but he had never shaken off the hacking cough by which he had been troubled for weeks now. During a prolonged bout of coughing one of his ribs had cracked.

'Does that mean you are out of it now for the rest of the trip?'

'Oh no, it's happened before and it got better. In another few days I should be O.K.!'

It was news to me that he had broken a rib earlier but now I realised the reason for his groans at night when he had shared the tent at Camp 2 and marvelled at his taciturnity.

'See you soon then,' and I continued to Camp 1.

When we arrived at the cave, Alan was in residence. Paul had left early in the day for Camp 3 and could be seen as a tiny speck of red on the way up to the West Shoulder. The cave was as familiar as home. Supplies were a little more sparse and the ceiling above the cooking area was blackened with the soot from an accident with a stove. Otherwise nothing had changed.

Alan busied himself melting snow and passing us drinks. He was still racked with frequent coughs and periodically, as if by auto-suggestion, I found that I too was succumbing to a bout. Once started, there was no escape. The cold, dry air compounded the irritation in the throat and the victim's body would be shaken by the hacking cough until randomly flung free of its spell. The nights at Base as well as on the mountain were often broken by staccato bursts of noise disturbing the sleep of the sufferer and all those around.

On the radio we heard that the Japanese had called a halt to their expedition and had started evacuating the mountain. In the little time that they had left they had no hope of the weather improving sufficiently to enable them to reach the summit. The Italians too were doubtful of their chances and with the Japanese withdrawing, the way up the icefall would be more difficult to maintain. Inevitably these items of news turned us to discussion of our own situation. If we did not, make some very definite progress on this attempt, we too would have little hope of climbing the mountain. Alan reckoned that we needed ten days of good weather if we were to stand a chance.

One improvement at Camp 1 had been the construction by Pete of a toilet. Previously we had used the bare hillside, digging a small hole as the need arose. Since the Lho La was rarely free from wind, 'going to the toilet' at any time, but especially at night, was a most undesirable ordeal. Our clothing was designed to allow the performance of the necessary functions by means of long zips that removed the need to undress completely. Nevertheless, a substantial area of the back and buttocks was still exposed. The operation was usually completed with the greatest of haste and one scuttled back to the sheltering cave feeling decidedly vulnerable and helpless against the demands of nature which could come at any time of day or night. I had got into the habit on expeditions of trying to establish a discipline in my bodily rhythms of only going to the toilet once a day, and that once in the morning. That way the whole business was completed along with all the other morning duties, otherwise it might mean disentangling oneself from harnesses and ropes and performing in even more precarious and unpleasant situations.

Even at the Lho La camp the problem was that whichever way one faced, the wind would always find the weak spot and even reaching a suitable place was a tricky manoeuvre with the risk of slipping or being blown down the slope outside the cave. We wore all of our clothes all the time, except boots, and the sensible thing to do was to dress completely in crampons, mitts and ice axe, but this conflicted with the tendency to want to rush outside, get the job over with quickly, and get back inside a warm sleeping bag once more.

So Pete, in a labour of love, had worked on his own for some hours digging a trench into the hillside and erecting a wall with blocks of snow on three sides of the trench. It was crude but effective and although the narrow track to the toilet became icy with use, most of the danger was taken out of this necessary function and Pete had the satisfaction of having built a toilet with the most splendid view in the world down into Tibet, overlooked by the summit of Everest and flanked by the walls of Nuptse.

Long after dark, lingering over the evening meal which was enlivened by some bacon from the exchange with the Italians, there was an unfamiliar rustling outside and. Paul startled us when he burst in out of the night. He looked haggard and morose. He had climbed two-thirds of the way up to Camp 3 before coming to a standstill. For him the expedition had gone on too long, he had no reserves of energy, and pains in his back due to an attack of hepatitis a few months earlier had grown unbearable. It was almost night when he had turned back and he had realised by the slow progress he had made that he would be able to achieve little from Camp 3 anyway.

In the morning Paul was still in pain and he regretfully explained his decision to continue on down to Base Camp. For him the expedition was over. He expected to be gone before we got down again and we made our goodbyes.

'Give everyone a ring when you get back home, tell them we won't be long, will you?'

Without Paul we were missing a solid, reliable workhorse. Throughout he had been willing to fit in and perform some of the least exciting but essential roles. I was sorry to see him go.

Alan left first, crossing the Lho La towards the ropes. Ade and I tested each other's sacks, gauging the weight of food and gear we were taking up to Camp 3. Thirty-five to forty pounds, they didn't feel heavy outside the cave but halfway to the bottom of the ropes they felt burdensome. We caught Alan up at the bergschrund where he was waiting to take some photographs. I loitered long enough to let Ade go in front – he seemed to have more energy than me – then I swung up the ropes after him and started the long, tedious haul to Camp 3, counting off each 150-foot length of rope as I passed the anchor point: one gone, thirty-five more ropes to go. Alan followed, always keeping at least one full rope length behind so that the weight of both of us was never on one anchor.

Ade soon outdistanced me, though Alan was going at the same pace. The three of us journeyed up hour after hour, separated by only a few hundred feet, without a word. The wind was strong enough to make us keep our hoods up, though the sky was clear. When I came through the trying stretches of the rock barrier, Ade was nowhere in sight. He had disappeared behind a rib of rock and from the top of it I could see jets of steam outlined by the sun which had not reached me yet revealing his location.

I never caught him up. Try as I might, my pace seemed slow, my sack a dead weight. When I reached the abandoned Camp 2, there were ten more rope lengths to go – almost there, only another hour and a half. Below, Alan had dropped back; he would be late.

The shadows were long down the Rongbuk glacier and the sun was setting before I arrived at Camp 3. I plunged inside down the long curving tunnel and grabbed the movie camera, an ancient Bolex. Outside, I filmed the boiling mass of clouds, spewing from the summit and catching the orange tints of the sinking sun. I was, awkward from the cold. The metal clung to my fingers as I risked using the camera without gloves and the warmth was sucked out of them by the cold casing. I made a clumsy mess of changing the film and tumbled back into the cave unsatisfied with my efforts but helpless from the pain of the cold in my hands.

It had taken me seven hours to reach Camp 3. Ade had done it in only five. Long after dark there was still no sign of Alan. The position of the cave precluded any sighting and only a descent of several hundred feet or a traverse across some precarious ice slopes would allow a view down to where he was last seen.

At 6 p.m., on the radio, Alan's voice came through from Camp 1. He too had ground to a halt well below Camp 3 and fearing benightment had descended while he still had strength and daylight left. We were relieved that he was safe but alarmed at the progressive weakening of the forces on the mountain. Alone again in this inhospitable ice chamber, Ade and I manoeuvred and shuffled like dogs in a new bed until we were ensconced in sleeping bags, food and stoves to hand and a pile of ice chunks ready for melting.

The hours of darkness in the Himalayas are long. In winter they were even more so, but sleep was harder to find. I was wary of taking any sleeping pills after the bad experiences the last time I was up. Consequently I passed a fitful night, my sleep disturbed for unknown reasons. Perhaps it was the cold draught through the cave, a particle of ice falling from the ceiling on to my face or contact with the ice-coated exterior of my sleeping bag as I turned over. Sometimes I was aware by his movements and altered breathing that Ade was awake too. I pestered him for the time. I had a watch, but to illuminate the face I had to press a button on the side. My fingers were too numb from the cold to do this.

Dawn's flat light filtered in through the walls of snow. The insulating mats on which we were sleeping were covered in a fine layer of snow which had settled from the air in the night. Ade made moves to light the small gas stove and start the day.

I confessed to him that I felt nauseous and headachey. The prospect of doing anything was not appealing but to decide to make no move upwards today would mean further demoralisation.

I got up to relieve myself and look outside. Beyond the crude curtain we now had over the entrance, the tunnel was lined with several inches of fresh snow. I crawled up it and poked my head out into a gale. Cloud was low and more snow was falling. I felt a guilty relief at the thought that we could justifiably have a day of rest. It would be too dangerous to go up on to the West Shoulder. At 8 a.m. we radioed down the situation. It was similarly wild at the Lho La, but Al and Brian were setting off from Base Camp to reach Camp 1.

Ade ministered to me all day making drinks and food. I was apologetic about my disability: 'I'm sorry I'm leaving you to do all the work.'

'That's O.K., you did it for me last time.'

It was -21 degrees Celsius inside the cave; the only advantage it had over the cave lower down was that here we had an inside toilet.

In civilisation one can hardly imagine passing a whole day and night lying next to a person with whom one is not emotionally involved. Little conversation passed between us, what little was to be said had already been reiterated many times in the weeks past. Making another cup of tea was an event as important as a dinner party, and took about as long to prepare. Gradually, through the administration of several pain killers and the intake of much liquid, my headache disappeared.

Even from Base Camp it was possible to misjudge the mountain. I sometimes used to wonder what could possibly stop us from putting one foot in front of the other, in making at least some progress. Lying in the cave was full of frustrations; we were drawn to satisfy our curiosity about the rest of the route, keen to advance a stage further. We could have gone outside, could have gone so far but without even discussing it we both knew the futility of such a gesture. A gesture as much demanded from within ourselves to ensure that we were not taking the soft option as from anything else.

I had spent a lot of time now with Ade and enjoyed the generous comradeliness of his company. He and his brother were quite different, I could see more clearly now, but different in a close way as if aspects of the same personality. This closeness seemed so strong that I was subconsciously surprised that they could perform independently of each other and made no obvious effort to make sure that they were teamed up. Ade was the more 'serious' of the two, often looking askance at the antics of his brother, who had a reputation for inadvertently wrecking things. Somehow a trenching tool had broken in his hands when digging a tent site at Camp 2; somehow the aerial on the master set of the radios had snapped when he was using it; somehow the syringe Pete had asked him to open in the tense moments round Wan Chup's sick bed had disintegrated in his hands. Al surfaced from each escapade with a self-mocking grin. One got the impression that Ade sometimes wanted to disown him.

Our food was a little better than it had been due to the discovery amongst the foods we had exchanged with the Italians of some easily cooked meals which tasted almost real. Tea and coffee had come to taste very acidic and the drink of preference was now one made from mineral salts and designed to help athletes. Whatever its benefits in that respect it made a refreshing change from tea and helped us consume the essential quantities of liquid.

The second night was as bad as the first. This time we both took a sleeping pill which Ade produced from his own little select pack of medicines. He assured me that they did not leave a nasty hangover like the others. We had too long to sleep though, and the effect of the pills wore off in the middle of the night, leaving us back playing the waiting game to see if we could move at dawn.

Both of us felt queasy by morning. We were unsure why. There was plenty of air in the cave and we had both been to such altitudes many times before. It is not unusual to have headaches the first time one reaches a certain height during an expedition, but after several weeks one can expect to be completely acclimatised. We could only assume that it was caused by constantly breathing extremely cold air and having a cold draught passing over our faces.

Ade made the breakfast but I was on my knees retching for a while before I felt well enough to take anything. The day was clear but still windy. If we were to make any progress at all on the mountain we would have to resign ourselves to climbing, if it was possible, in the wind. We radioed down our intention of taking some gear up on to the West Shoulder to assess conditions.

We took some coils of rope and digging tools each, intending to make a dump of gear along the ridge, thus easing the next day's work when we expected to go right through to the site for Camp 4. Since our loads were not too heavy we took a movie camera each, Ade the big, heavy Bolex and I the smaller, cartridge-loading Autoload. Mike was not to come any higher than the Lho La and now, in the absence of the professional, we felt less inhibited about our untutored efforts and also more responsibility to take film.

The Autoload was easy to handle. There were few controls and the cartridges were readily slotted in, even with mittened hands. A cartridge only lasted for sixty seconds though, hardly enough time to get into the rhythm of filming. Ade was off in front again and I tried to capture the ecstatic view of him silhouetted against the sun with streamers of wind-driven snow snaking down over the glistening ice and past his feet. There was no way of checking our results until we arrived back in Britain – it was a matter of shoot it and see.

Sixty seconds seemed a long time at altitude until I checked the film counter. The film had snapped with the cold. Without much regret, having tried to do my duty, I put the camera away. Anyway, as I reached the rounded plateau I was occupied more and more with trying to keep my balance against the fierce gusts.

Ade was sitting on the same lone piece of black rock we had come across on our first visit here. He had the weighty Bolex pressed to his eye recording my erratic gait. For hand-held filming it is best not to breathe while the finger is actually on the trigger to avoid camera shake. Any effort to hold one's breath at altitude for more than a few seconds brought on a rapid, panicky gulping for air. The oxygen was already scarce enough without cutting it off completely. As I reached him, Ade pulled the camera away from his face. A white streak of frost-burn lined his nose where the cold metal of the camera case had frozen into place. Ade did not know it had happened till I shouted above the noise of the wind to take care. His whole face was numb and he would not feel any pain from the frost-burn until it warmed up. More of a perfectionist than me, he had taken his goggles off to see more clearly through the viewfinder.

We soaked in the splendid panorama. Communication was hardly possible. The wind was far stronger than the first time we had come up to this point and to go further would be risky. This was a risk we felt we would have to take if we were going to get any further. Roped together would be the only way to advance, giving ourselves a chance of safeguarding each other against any slip. Sometimes I looked at the rest of the route as if it were just a short step, sometimes it seemed infinite. The only way to treat it was a little bit at a time.

We turned to go back, dumping the gear beside the rock; the incongruous spade, proof even against Al's latent destructiveness, was thrust into the snow to mark the spot. We believed we could make headway against the wind and would return next day, with luck with reinforcements, and make our way right along the ridge.

Back at Camp 3 we were puzzled to find no sign of any new arrivals. By dark still no one had arrived and the clear skies had gone, replaced by turbulent, snow-filled clouds.

We expected an explanation on the radio call but nothing came through from Camp 1. From Base Camp we heard the alarming news that John had not recovered from his sickness and had left for home with Paul. Pete was on the radio and he explained that he had found John to have a chest infection as well as dysentery. John was unable to eat and had decided to leave for lower altitudes rather than grow progressively weaker trying to fight the illness in Base Camp.

A quarter of the strength of the team had thus vanished. Logically there were many reasons for Paul and John to have left but it was a savage blow and seemed to mock our attempts at getting any further. There was no blame to attach to their decision to leave, Pete himself had been adamant on the radio that John stood no chance of recovering, but with the arrogance of the fit I did feel a wordless frustration and fought hard within myself to maintain optimism. Their departure, however, compounded by the failure of anyone to arrive, aroused grave disquiet in our minds. For a couple of hours after dark Ade and I chewed over what was going on and whether up at Camp 3 we were as isolated and out on a limb as we felt. If no one was able to reach Camp 3, what prospect did we stand on our own? Certainly we could probably reach the site for Camp 4 and start digging a cave, but apart from the strain of working unsupported at such an altitude for several days we would soon run out of food and have to descend.

We resolved to do some straight talking next morning on the radio. If no one was coming up, was the risk involved in going further along the West Ridge worth taking? This night too passed with fitful sleep but this time it was for other reasons than the unpleasant physical conditions by which we were surrounded.

11   STRAIGHT TALKING

Al came on the radio for the morning call. Ade spoke to him. It was the best possible pairing for a dialogue. Intimate as they were, with no means of subterfuge, these two could be more blunt and more open than most people ever could be to their closest friends.

Ade made the first call: 'Camp 3 to Lho La, come in please.'

Al replied 'Lola,' as he used to pronounce it, 'to Camp 3, hearing you loud and clear. How do you hear me? Over.'

'Loud and clear. What is going on? Why has no one come up? Do people intend to come up? Over.'

'It was too windy yesterday and no one here feeling is good. It is too windy again today to cross Lola.'

'Look, we went up to the West Shoulder yesterday to see what it was like. It was windy but we should be able to get further. If we can go up there in the wind you should be able to get up here.'

'Well, I don't feel well at all and Brian and Alan here have doubts about their effectiveness even if they can reach Camp 3.'

The exchange was punctuated by pauses waiting for the 'Over', to mark the end of one message. Only one party could speak at a time as the transmit button cut out sound reception. The tendency to interject comments into conversation as it went along was thus thwarted and in an crucial exchange like this there was much frustration in waiting to speak.

Ade said: 'If no one comes up to Camp 3 they won't ever get acclimatised to the altitude. It's best to come up and have a day's rest here if necessary instead of waiting at the Lho La to feel fit. That's 3,000 feet lower. Is anyone going to come or not?'

'The feeling here is that you are being over-optimistic.'

'Look, we went up there yesterday specifically to find out and we reckon it is worth trying even in the wind if we are roped up.'

'Brian suggests that you and Joe go to establish Camp 4 if you think it possible; people can then come up to give a hand.'

'We need help now. We need at least the moral support of knowing that we aren't sticking our necks out going along that ridge, which won't be easy, only to find we've done it for nothing.'

'If you two doubt your ability to get along there, and you're going better than any of us, what chance has anyone else got?'

'Look, it's black and white. We can't do everything on our own. If no one comes up there is no point in us going on.'

'Don't try to put the onus on us. If you want to give it a go getting to Camp 4 then do so.'

The artificially clipped manner of the dialogue also lent bluntness to the comments. With anyone else making this exchange there would have been the risk of arousing hostility by such sharp retorts. However, the anger which I knew Ade felt and which he was trying to express to his brother was curtailed by the formalities of radio talk. Ade swore for me to hear as his brother's monotone replies came out of the radio. There was a clear polarisation between the two camps. Brian described the radio exchange as heard at Camp 1:

> The three of us, Alan, Al and myself, lay side by side in the ice cave, surrounded by a jumble of clothing and gear.
>
> Alan was huddled up, his down-suited body protruding from his sleeping bag, a morose expression on his face. Al had the walkie-talkie in his hands. I broke into the exchange which Al was having with his brother: 'What the hell do they mean – need our support? What are we sat in this ice box for if it's not support? Let me talk to them, Al!'
>
> 'No, I just want to finish talking to Ade. They must realise that there is no way we can get to the top now.'

I agreed with him: 'Yes, can't they see that with Paul and John on their way home, Pete with a broken rib, you with a bad chest, me and Alan totally demoralised, we just haven't got enough people left to make an attempt on the summit?'

Suddenly Alan burst out angrily. 'Give me the radio! Lho La to Camp 3, do you receive me? Over.'

'Ade from 3. Receiving at strength one. Please repeat. Over.'

Alan twiddled with knobs and the aerial before shouting into the radio and receiving Ade's reply. 'Receiving you strength four. If nobody will come up to help us we cannot continue. We need support. If you can't come up, we will come down. Over.'

Aside from the radio, Alan responded with more impatience: 'What the hell are they talking about? We've been sat here for seven days out of the last ten. We've had three good days in the last month when we could climb along the West Ridge. We need eight continuous days of good weather to get to the top. I'm bored with lying here day after day, feeling cold, ill and hungry.'

'Lho La to Camp 3, Alan here!' he shouted into the radio, pausing between each word so that the message was emphatic. 'If ... the ... weather ... gets ... better ... we ... will ... come ... up ... No ... point ... otherwise ... Just ... to ... get ... tired ... at ... Camp ... 3 ... You ... are ... only ... two ... strong ... enough ... to ... push ... above ... Camp ... 3 ... Over.'

'Camp 3 to Lho La. Sorry, reception bad. Please repeat. Over.'

'If ... weather ... gets ... better ... will ... come ... up ... Over.'

With that, Alan's voice finally cracked and he croaked in a whisper: 'Oh Christ, somebody else try

to get some sense out of them,' and he finished with
a fit of coughing and retching.

Suddenly Pete broke in: 'Hello Camp 3 and Camp 1, Pete speaking from Base, can I add a few comments? Over.'

'Hearing you loud and clear ... Over.'

Pete continued: 'There seems to be a crucial discussion going
on. I know I have got a broken rib but my vote is for pressing on.
I'm not saying we can do it now at this late stage but I think we
should stick it out for another few days. Things might just work
out for us?'

I took the radio: 'Hello, Joe speaking. Those are my feelings too.
Time is short but we might as well use it. We do need some support.'

Pete: 'Could you and Ade just stay up another few days?'

'We could stay up a few more days but I don't fancy sticking my
neck out not knowing what is going on.'

'Can't you give a demonstration of what is still possible by going
along to Camp 4? That might change the whole attitude.'

'We gave a bloody demonstration yesterday. What do you think
this is, a circus? I don't think it's time for demonstrations. Everyone
at Camp 1 seems to disagree that there's any chance left of us getting up the mountain in the weather we are stuck with now. If they
can't get up now, what is the likelihood of them coming up in three
days' time? We aren't putting the onus on them of calling a halt –
the onus is on them. We are getting nowhere with this conversation. No one is saying what they really mean. Before coming to
any hasty decision, let's think about it. Let's have another radio
call at eleven to give everyone time to think things over.

We switched off. Ade and I relapsed into a glum silence. We
both knew each other's minds. We wanted to go on even though
we knew there remained little chance. The most rewarding
achievements only come from succeeding against the greatest
odds. On the other hand we had more than the weather to con-
tend with. Ade and I had been lucky in escaping most of the ills
which had bedevilled the expedition and when one is fit it is hard
to comprehend how great problems can be, both mental and

physical, for someone who is sick. There had been a lot of debilitating sickness and Everest in winter was showing no mercy to the sick. Brian had just recovered from yet another attack of dysentery. Alan, a skeleton of his former self, could hardly be understood over the radio, his voice was so hoarse, and now Al too had developed a chest infection. Sickness makes everything seem so much more difficult and even were it possible for anyone to drive himself on, the result could be fatal.

Ade was convinced that there would be no change of opinion. The date was 31 January. We had been on the mountain for nearly two months. The constant cold, bitter, brutal winds and snowstorms had steadily eroded our strength and resources. Perhaps Everest was too big an objective to tackle so early in this new phase of Himalayan exploration; the problems were far different and less obvious than in other seasons. I did feel in one part of my mind that there would be some relief in giving up this interminable struggle; the mental and physical strain of sustaining such effort over two months is extreme and no matter what the disappointment at not reaching the top there would be the pleasure of having survived, the satisfaction of knowing that we had battled with Everest at the worst time of the year and had not lost anyone or had any serious accidents.

While waiting for 11 a.m. and the decision, we made another drink and started sorting out which gear we would take down.

Outside only the eyes of an optimist could see the weather as being reasonable, and for the past month, apart from two days, we had known only storm and wind. There was no indication that we could expect any better in the next few days.

At 11 a.m. we opened up radio communication again.

'Hello Camp 1 and Base, are you listening? What is the position now? Are there any new thoughts on the situation? Over.'

Pete came on the radio and there was a dialogue between him and Camp 1. Brian gave his view of it:

Pete's voice was enthusiastic, I could tell, even over the radio:

> 'Pete to Camp 1 and 3. I think that whilst we still
> have time left and people on the mountain we

should keep trying at least for another week. Perhaps we'll get a spell of good weather. Can't anyone from Camp 1 get up to Camp 3? Over.'

I resented Pete sitting at Base Camp and trying to tell us what to do. 'Thanks, Pete, but winds are too strong today. Could not get up the ropes, but see no point in going up anyway if there is going to be just more bad weather.'

Alan sat up from a bout of coughing and, echoing my own and Al's sentiments, said into the radio: 'Get lost, Pete, you're just complicating things.'

Pete obviously did not hear this at Base Camp and Al commented after some thought: 'I suppose Pete's got just as much right to his opinion as everyone else.'

'Yes,' I said, 'it's just that discussing the end of a trip which you've worked on for the past six months, over a radio with poor reception, does not lend itself to friendly conversation.'

Joe's voice cut in with icy finality: 'If you don't come up from Camp 1 in support we might as well come down. Over.'

At Camp 3 we heard Al reply: 'If you want to stay up we are prepared to back you but there doesn't seem much point.'

'Is anyone coming up?'

'No one is really fit enough to.'

The refusal to come to the point and the oral fencing round the real issue continued. Ade groaned. He left the radio on 'receive' and we heard Pete come in again from Base Camp and conduct a long dialogue with Camp 1 on the same lines as the earlier discussion. 'To me,' Ade said: 'Nothing has changed. We might as well face it. They're never going to come up. By support we're talking about different things. I think they mean they'll be praying for us. They can't help being ill, but wait till I see our kid. I think this winter game has been too much for everyone.'

There was a look of resignation on his face and he started to stuff gear into a rucksack for descent. I lay back, listening to the discussion flying back and forth between Camp 1 and Base Camp. Pete was putting up a spirited argument for maintaining the impetus. The response from Camp 1 was that he was misjudging the situation on the mountain and that he himself was not of much use anyway with a broken rib. The discussion went on and on. Half an hour passed and Ade was ready to leave. The attitudes of everyone concerned were exactly the same as they had been at the start.

'There isn't going to be any change,' said Ade. 'I'm going to set off down. Might as well try and get to Base Camp in one go. See you later.' He pushed his sack up the tunnel and disappeared.

I too busied myself retrieving valuable pieces of camera gear and sleeping bags. When I was ready to leave I waited a while longer, listening to the still raging discourses. Still no change, and I scrambled up the tunnel for the last time, turning my thoughts to the consolations – no more grim nights in that hole, the gradual return to civilisation and comfort.

My rucksack was exceedingly heavy. Both Ade and I were taking down the maximum possible knowing that that it was unlikely that anyone else would now be coming up. As I swung down the ropes on the steepening slopes back to the Lho La, I had to fight the wind throwing me off balance and I asked myself how realistic I had been in declaring that it would have been possible to make further progress in such weather. Did I really think we stood any chance now of getting up the mountain or did I simply not want to lose face by capitulating to a more rational assessment of our situation? I did not know the answer myself. The way down to the level plateau of the Lho La seemed interminable. I could see Ade, far below, and a tiny speck which left Camp 1 on its way down. I sank to my knees to rest at every anchor point, longing to be out of the wearying wind.

The plateau of the Lho La was only a change, not a relief. The wind knocked me back and forth and I paused frequently, waiting for a lull before staggering on a few steps. The final slight rise up to Camp 1 took forever. I felt self-conscious under the scrutiny of Alan who was waiting at the cave entrance with a drink ready.

Al had already gone down. Alan and Brian were staying at Camp 1 to pack everything up and clear as much gear as possible. Ade left as soon as I arrived and I hastened after him.

I dumped my sack halfway down as my legs kept giving way beneath me and once clear of the roped areas I knew I could easily retrieve it the next day. At the camp I walked into a barrage of questions by a camera and microphone from the film crew wanting instant reactions to the decision to call off the expedition.

Ade was involved in an angry dispute with his brother. 'Bloody support,' I heard him say. 'You couldn't carry a shopping basket to a supermarket, let alone a sack of gear up this hill.' Al looked crestfallen and apologetic. Harder words could fly between these two than between any of the rest of us, and Ade was clearing his system of all the resentment that had built up over the last few days before the task of winding up the expedition should take precedence and form us into a working team again.

12   THE WIND UP

Our postal system had finally shown a flaw. A mail bag had gone missing – a multitude of letters and cards, ninety minutes of film, $300 in travellers' cheques. We had sent the mail bag in question at the beginning of January and it had taken a month for it to be reported to us that it had not arrived in Kathmandu. None of us kept track of to whom we had written or when; that mail was irretrievable. Mike Shrimpton, professional to the last, had a note of every roll of film he had sent off, and dutifully he set off back up to the Lho La to retake as much of the missing footage as he could. There was much coming and going at this time retrieving gear from the mountain and Mike went up with Brian and Pete. Pete showed an unsuspected propensity for conservation, even going back up to Camp 3 once to rescue what bits Ade and I had been unable to carry down. Some things were too bulky but rather than abandon them Pete made a couple of large bundles and trundled them down the 3,000-foot slope to the Lho La, rescuing the remains much later when he himself arrived.

The Japanese and Italians were also in the process of dismantling their Base Camps. Hordes of porters and Sherpas arrived, invading our solitude and picking like looters at every unattended piece of equipment or box of food. They had long grown accustomed to expeditions winding up and abandoning much valuable gear so that they have come to take it that they have a right to anything left around. These were Sherpas in a different light from what we had seen before and the camp had the feel of a beleaguered garrison as we cleared up, burning rubbish and packing our belongings ready for departure.

Mr Singh became ill and did not appear from his tent for three days. The only sound emanating from that direction was indistinguishable between singing and groaning. Graham, camped beside him, reported hearing the same sounds throughout the night and believed the strain of nearly three months in the mountains was beginning to unbalance our shy Liaison Officer.

Finally we left, the familiar smell of juniper wood smoke from the Italian camp trailing after us for a long time. The chaos of packing, loading yaks, arguing over rates and weights, all compressed into a straggling line of ponderous animals as we made our way downwards into deeper snow where the wind had not blown with such force.

In only a short time Everest slipped behind the wall of Nuptse and our self-imposed exile was over. I had a feeling of freedom, of walking unencumbered by any constraints; alive again with no dangers ahead to face up to; alive with dreams still intact, with a goal to aim for. This had been a punishing experience. We had kept in control, we were all returning without loss of life or limb in the party, but in two months we had grown to accept as normal the most harrowing living conditions we had known and had tried to climb the highest mountain in the world by its most difficult route. The Japanese, with a different style of expedition on a different route, had been turned back from a similar height on the same mountain. Some of our party thought that Everest, in winter, without oxygen and especially by the West Ridge, was impossible. The time needed to be spent on the mountain had left us weak and unable to combat illnesses. The winds had been relentless and it was often physically impossible to move in them. There was no doubt that we had every justification in retreating before we found ourselves fighting for our lives with no physical or material resources left, but the objective remained. Perhaps we needed this expedition to learn what was necessary for success. Few people dare to say that any problem in mountaineering now is impossible to solve; failure only enhances the prestige of the objective. After dropping somewhat in esteem in recent years due to the numerous ascents of the mountain, Everest was now restored to its pre-eminent position. Winter mountaineering in the Himalayas opens a new chapter in the sport with the ascent of Everest as its greatest prize.

We made our way over several days to Lukla, the air strip from which we were to fly out. The lower valleys, with trees laden with snow, had a more familiar look of winter than the Base Camp we had left where the barren wastes change little with the arrival of more snow.

We met a Sherpa, 'Long' Tensing, who had been with the Burgess twins on an earlier expedition: 'Success?'

'No.'

'Members all O.K.?'

'Yes.'

'On Everest that is success!'

In Kathmandu the pace of life changed. Months away from modern communications and we were like savages undergoing culture shock. The first night back and we found ourselves at a party in an embassy house. They were all the 'beautiful people' of Kathmandu but we were ill at ease. Lost in the mêlée of noise and strangers, we clung together for reassurance, unable to make conversation or relate to what was happening.

We were eating in a restaurant once when a shaven-headed girl, dressed in the purple robes of the Buddhist faith, walked up to our table. She looked from one Burgess twin to the other.

'Which one?' she said, and Al, his gaping mouth demonstrating his bewilderment, recognised the girl he had met on the way in.

The twins stayed behind to forward all our baggage. The rest of us, gradually separating off from the close-knit group we had become, boarded the plane for home. I was not prepared for it. A million strings were drawing me back but those strings came from another side of a wall and did not have any meaning until I should be amongst them again. As we approached London I felt a sense of nervousness as if I had become estranged from life at home and that back in the mountains we had left some unfinished business.

ACKNOWLEDGEMENTS

This is a personal account of the British Everest Winter Expedition. There are as many different facets to the story as there were people on the venture. However, in putting together this account, I received substantial contributions from Brian Hall, Allen Jewhurst, Paul Nunn, John Porter, Pete Thexton and Mike Shrimpton. I am indebted to Christopher Falkus of Eyre Methuen and George Greenfield of John Farquharson for their enthusiasm and Ann Mansbridge for her painstaking editorial work and rigorous discipline which kept me to a tight schedule. To my colleagues who made it possible to complete the book in the time available, and to Jill Hield who typed the manuscript with most helpful speed and efficiency, I owe a particular debt of gratitude.

Bass Ltd, New Era Laboratories, the Mount Everest Foundation and the British Mountaineering Council all provided financial support and many companies, particularly Mountain Equipment and Berghaus, provided material support, all of which made the expedition possible in the first place.

To these, and to the team above all, I owe thanks.

Joe Tasker
Hope, Derbyshire
1982

ABOUT THE AUTHOR

Joe Tasker was one of Britain's foremost mountaineers. He was a pioneer of lightweight, 'alpine-style' climbing in the Greater Ranges and had a special talent for writing. He died, with his friend Peter Boardman, high on Everest in 1982 while attempting the previously unclimbed North-East Ridge. Their deaths marked the end of a remarkable era in British mountaineering.

Born in Hull in 1948, Joe began rock climbing in his teens. Drawn to mountaineering, he made many remarkable ascents in the Alps, including the first British winter ascent of the North Face of the Eiger, before moving to the Greater Ranges. Here, Joe pioneered routes of extreme technical difficulty in a bold, alpine-style – at a time when huge expeditions and siege tactics were still the mountaineering norm.

Peter and Joe left two legacies. One was their great endeavour, their climbs on high peaks with bold, lightweight innovative methods; the second is the books they wrote and left behind. Both had developed a special talent for writing. Joe's first book *Everest the Cruel Way* is an exciting account of his winter attempt on Everest and his second book, *Savage Arena*, was finished just before he left for Everest in 1982. Both have become mountaineering classics.

The Boardman Tasker Award for Mountain Literature was established in Pete and Joe's honour, and is presented annually to the author or co-authors of an original work which has made an outstanding contribution to mountain literature. For more information about the Boardman Tasker Award, visit: *www.boardman-tasker.com*